C000281298

Jules Middleton has worked in is now a vicar in the Church of you don't let that put you off!) husband who works full time, a half-hearted runner and a full-time lover of the sea, which she enjoys regularly as she lives on the edge of the South Downs. Jules also writes freelance and via her blog *Apples of Gold*, which has been nominated for several Premier Digital Awards and was awarded Runner Up Most Inspiring Leadership Blog of the year in 2017. She appears regularly on radio, including BBC Radio Sussex.

Twitter: @redjules Instagram: JulesMiddleton Facebook: Jules Middleton100

'I have had the privilege of walking with Jules from her first steps back to faith, her journey to a vocation and then had the joy of ordaining her. The characteristic joy, creativity and flair that makes her such an excellent priest runs throughout this amusing, poignant and searingly honest book. A winsome combination of personal story and theological reflection, it demonstrates very clearly why women in the priesthood are such a gift to the Church.'
Rt Revd Richard Jackson, Bishop of Lewes and Bishop-designate of Hereford

'Down to earth, honest and practical, this book debunks so many myths about ministry and parenting. While I have never been ordained, as an itinerant woman in ministry, I identify whole-heartedly with some of Jules's challenges but also her passion. Some-how, we have to get real and we have to get intentional about women fulfilling their potential in ministry settings. This book is a valuable handbook to have in that quest and will be a great encouragement to those who also have families to consider.'
Cathy Madavan, speaker, author and Kyria Network board member

'Jules Middleton's impassioned and authentic voice is one that the Church of England needs to listen carefully to in relation to women's ministry. Reading her book was enlightening, alarming and inspiring. Written in an accessible, engaging way and peppered with practical insights, biblical nuggets and relevant stories, I hope that it greatly encourages those women already in ministry and perhaps gives a holy nudge to those reluctant to push the door, for whatever reason. This book is a timely reminder that God calls us as we are – thank heavens for that!'
Revd Matt Woodcock, Pioneer Minister and author

'Jules writes with insight, humour and sensitivity. She also writes with honesty and integrity, meaning that this book will make you laugh and cry along with her. Not just for ministry mums.'
Revd Kate Bottley, broadcaster

'This book is a thoughtful and practical exploration of the challenges and triumphs of juggling ordained ministry as a mum, borne out of personal experience. In a space where it can be hard to find other role models, the various personal reflections and testimonies in the book are really helpful. As Jules says, "this juggle is real" and, if you're attempting or even contemplating juggling ministry and motherhood, it will be a helpful and empathetic companion on your journey.'
Dr Kate Middleton, Assistant Pastor at Zeo Church, Hitchin, and Director of the Mind and Soul Foundation

'A fantastic book by Jules Middleton: funny, moving and deeply practical. A wonderful, witty account of the joys and challenges of combining being a mum and a priest, peppered with wise advice – a must-read for ministry mums and their congregations.'
Isabelle Hamley, Chaplain to the Archbishop of Canterbury

BREAKING THE MOULD

Learning to thrive as a ministry mum

Jules Middleton

First published in Great Britain in 2020

Society for Promoting Christian Knowledge
36 Causton Street
London SW1P 4ST
www.spck.org.uk

British Library Cataloguing-in-Publication Data
A catalogue record for this book is available from the British Library

ISBN 978–0–281–08327–5
eBook ISBN 978–0–281–08328–2

1 3 5 7 9 10 8 6 4 2

Typeset by Manila Typesetting Company
First printed in Great Britain by Jellyfish Print Solutions
Subsequently digitally reprinted in Great Britain

eBook by Manila Typesetting Company

Produced on paper from sustainable forests

Contents

Foreword by Revd Dr Sharon Prentis   ix

Acknowledgements   xiii

Introduction   1

1 Unmumsy and unvicary: Hanging on to your identity by your fingernails   9

2 Moulds and hammers: Smashing the way it's always been done   23

3 Becoming Mum: The early years   39

4 Endless expectations: And not giving in to them   53

5 Formation or transformation? Being intentional about change   67

6 Sustainable sacrifice: Not offering yourself on the altar of ministry   81

7 Prayer and Prosecco: Getting rest and recreation   97

8 Distraction and defeat: When it all gets too much   113

Summary   129

Bibliography   137

Further reading and resources   141

Foreword

I have always been puzzled by the phrase used as the title of the poem 'The hand that rocks the cradle is the hand that rules the world', by William Ross Wallace. Although the intent is to praise motherhood as a force for positive change in the world, there were times in my own experience when that seemed far from the truth. My own world was an inadequately tuned balancing act of trying to fit more activity into ever-decreasing time without succumbing to 'mother-guilt', which often followed hot on the heels of any sense of satisfaction.

As a clergy spouse, before eventually becoming ordained myself, there was always a conflict between wanting to do the best for the family and wanting to do the best for God. This conflict only became heightened even more during and after training. It wasn't until much later that I realised doing the best for God *was* doing the best for the family: they were both the same thing. It was the external pressures, unrealistic expectations I placed on myself and the views of others, that heightened my sense of not being all that! Now, years later, reflecting on the challenges of co-parenting and ministry, it was often the case that we worked it out as we went along rather than followed any predetermined plan. Our approach was a type of 'lyrical improvisation' in response to life changes as we moved parishes, dioceses and jobs – the melody of the journey being characterised by different schools, playmates, friends, parishioners, challenging issues and life-changing events. We said hello to brand new family members and sad goodbyes to loved ones. A whole spectrum of life experiences became intertwined with this thing called 'ministry'.

Back then, books on family life and ministry were non-existent. Money was tight so doing paid work, alongside the demands that come from 'living on the job' and a stipend, was a necessity. We improvised our way through, learning as we went along and catching insights from the wisdom of others.

The combination of being a black woman from a working-class background in church leadership also meant the reality was that I had to work twice as hard to get half as far. It is a little less challenging now, but I have learnt over the years that God's loving grace allows you to inhabit the moment and gives you the momentum needed to press through. Then there's the wisdom gained from listening to the stories of others and observing how they navigate the complexities of their vocational journey. I am indebted to those who instinctively knew when to listen, when to offer a cup of tea or gave the hug that was needed.

Inevitably there are times when things do not work out as hoped, when it feels dreadful; those are the times when we learn and grow, eventually coming to understand that we are becoming. The African American writer Maya Angelou said, 'We delight in the beauty of the butterfly, but rarely admit the changes it has gone through to achieve that beauty.' I look back over those years with awe, reflecting on how swiftly they have passed and how much has changed. Our daughter has now grown up and we gaze on the last two decades as a family too with wonder and incredulity.

This book captures the highs and lows in ministry. It's a book that I wish had been written over twenty years ago when our daughter was a toddler in a vicarage. The wise insights and hilarious descriptions are familiar to all. It is for those of us who wonder if we can navigate the journey, who worry about the impact on our children and closest relationships, who question our capacity and wonder if we are good enough. What will be found within these pages is honest wisdom and the overwhelming message that it is OK to be yourself. More importantly, that you have been uniquely created and equipped to undertake what is required. It is not so much about 'having it all', as a popular book title proclaimed a few years ago, but bringing all of you to what you are called to be.

Sharon Prentis

Acknowledgements

I feel it is somewhat ironic that, as I write this, I am contemplating the removal of nits from my daughter's hair. As a ministry mum, there are regularly opposing pulls on my time and the weighing up of which one wins is an ongoing lesson. I say this before you read on because I want you to know that I am by no means an expert mother. I am simply trying to keep going – in motherhood *and* ministry – without messing up my kids or my church too much. Thankfully, I do neither alone. Similarly, this book would not have been put together without a heap of input from others: families, partners, children, ministers, all sharing their experiences and their ideas. Here's where I get to say thank you to them, so prepare yourselves while I launch into an Oscars-style speech moment . . .

To Amber, Elliott and Poppy, who have brought me overwhelming pride and joy from the moment you were born, have made me belly laugh and occasionally sob uncontrollably, who are so much a product of your parents, but also totally your own people. To say this book would be nothing without you is of course true, but seems a gigantic understatement about your impact on my life. You challenge me to rethink my opinions, never cease to inspire me and make me proud every day just by being you. I love you (and, yes, I am crying as I write this, you know it).

To my friends and wider family who have, frankly, not seen me for months as I've spent every spare hour tapping away on the keyboard; thanks for being understanding. To Mum, the first working woman I knew, thanks for showing me it's OK to be ambitious as a woman (but also for the best roast potatoes in the world!) Thanks to you and Dad for putting up with my teenage angst and for being my cheerleaders through good and bad; love you. Thanks to you both and Juliet for being amazing grandparents – you enrich the lives of our kids in so many ways. I am so thankful for wonderful friends, especially at The Point and TRINITY, and, among others, Julie, Sarah, Iain, Andy, Stu, Nikki and John; you guys are always in my heart. To the Shady Bitches – you make Lewes life so much fun. To Sarah, a remarkable prayer warrior, for walking with me (literally – we love you, Lancing beach) through all kinds of seasons that no one else knows about; you are an amazing friend.

To all those who have inspired me and encouraged me on my journey in ministry, thank you. To the Bolney Mums, the Christian Bloggers – particularly Lesley, Anita and Rachel in the early days; to the tutors who showed me women in ministry could thrive: Clare and Georgie particularly; and ministers whose work I've followed but never met: Nadia Bolz-Weber, you give me so much hope for the Church. To those I've studied and worked with: the SEITE/ St Augustine's crew and IME pals, thanks for sharing the laughter and tears. And to my spiritual director, Jan, who always draws me back to Jesus – thank you for your wisdom.

To the 'Clergy Mummies' Facebook community – you were the initial motivation for this book. You provide a place where ministry mums can really support one another and I don't know what I'd do without you all. Particular thanks go to those who have provided their stories to encourage others through this book: Caroline, Helen C., Jac, Katie, Jo P., Ruth, Helen W-C., Ramona, Jo R. and all those whose experiences are scattered throughout this book.

To Elizabeth, my commissioning editor at SPCK, who saw my idea and just got it – this book is only what it is because of your input and belief in me.

And now for the guys. To the dads who are ministers fighting for their own rights, to Andy Griffiths and men like him who are actively championing women in ministry. To Will, James and Steve – three amazing ordained men who have walked with me at various stages of the ministry journey. Thank you all for being part of the solution.

And to Phil, my partner in this bonkers life. I have no idea what I would do without you; you are my team and I thank God for you every day. Here's to the next 20 years; I love you. You're only usurped in the headline act of this list by Jesus, who always gets the last word.

Jesus, thank you for loving me as I am. For never losing sight of me, even when I'm running in the opposite direction; thank you for believing in me and calling me to your Church, even though I don't feel like I belong. Thank you for the cross.

Amen.

It is our duty as men and women
to proceed as though the limits of
our abilities do not exist.

(PIERRE TEILHARD DE CHARDIN)

Introduction

Borrowing a chocolate fountain for a party of six-year-old boys may not have been my best decision ever. I'm not sure my kitchen curtains will ever be the same and, for years, every time I made a cup of tea, I saw the one impossible-to-reach chocolate stain taunting me from the corner of the ceiling. You see, that was the day of 'the phone call' – the point of no going back – the DDO (Diocesan Director of Ordinands) calling me up in the midst of this chocolate mayhem to summon me to a meeting about discerning a call to ordained ministry.

Exiting the kitchen, I desperately legged it up the stairs to a quieter room, all the while praying the fountain would survive and that my heavy breathing from running up the stairs would not alert the DDO to my unsuitability for ministry. In that moment I panicked, a range of unwelcome thoughts running through my mind at speed. What on earth am I doing? I can't be a vicar; I have a job I am quite happy with, thank you very much. God can't possibly be calling me. Look at me – I've got a chocolate strawberry squished into my T-shirt. Oh God, please make him tell me to bugger off. I don't want this. 'MUUUUUUUUM!' A screech from the kitchen wafted up the stairs. God, please don't let him have heard that. Oh God, *help!*

I still imagine that, while I flapped, filled with terror, God was sitting somewhere, on a celestial cloud, laughing hysterically. Because, of course, the DDO did not tell me to bugger off and I am now, in fact, a vicar. Many times, I have looked back at that moment and wondered at the wisdom of God, bringing *that* phone call into *that* moment and reminding me time and again through *that* memory that I am just as much a mum and a wife as I am a minister. These days, life is one continual round of juggling a metaphorical chocolate fountain with ministry and attempting to avoid strawberries getting squished into my now *clerical* shirt, and I'm not alone in this.

At the time of writing, I am one of around 6,000 female clergy in the UK. Yes, you read that right – there are 6,000 of us. And yet, we still seem to be a source of intrigue, mystery even – 'What, you're a real vicar?' 'Are you like the Vicar of Dibley?' 'Is that even allowed?' Amazing as it might seem, women have now been priests in the UK for over 25 years. Female church leaders are not just in the Church of England either; ministry mums cross a range of denominations and a variety of leadership roles. Between us, at times we have taken different roles: bishops, moderators and presidents; youth pastors and preachers; chaplains in all kinds of interesting places, including to the Queen and the Speaker of the House of Commons; we are in the military, the workplace, hospitals and schools – and, of course, lots of us are also mums, juggling the realities of work and life, which for me, is usually by the skin of my teeth.

In our case, we have always been a working family, whether from necessity, desire or calling. Our three children have grown up with the reality of after-school clubs, childminders, a fair amount of time spent with grandparents and of 'working from home'. My husband often reminds our now teenage son of the time he wandered into a room announcing, 'Daaaaad, I need a pooooooo', singing over his dad's conference call! As my family will feature throughout the pages of this book, it might be helpful to introduce us properly here. There's me, Jules, a priest in the Church of England, a creative type (I used to be an artist), with a love of the sea, a half-hearted runner and a bit of a freelance writer. Now, I should say at this point, I probably overshare too often, am fiercely protective of my family, can get a bit ranty at times (OK, very) and have been known to drop the odd F bomb after a glass of wine or two – and a few of those have been drunk during the writing of this book.

In addition, I firmly believe that God encompasses male *and* female, so I always try to use non-gender-specific language for God

2

(though, as many of us find, age-old cultural norms die hard). For the same reason, Bible references come from the NRSV (unless otherwise stated), as it is more gender-inclusive than the other versions.

Please don't be offended, wound up or put off reading on for any of those reasons. I still love Jesus and his Church and am passionate about encouraging women in ministry, so I hope that I can encourage you too.

I am married to Phil, who works full time, mostly in London, doing something security related that, to be honest, I have never really understood. He's a bit of a muso and ~~loves~~ *attempts* to surf. We share everything at home, from school runs and food shopping to cleaning the lav and ironing (OK, that's a lie; he does all the ironing).

We've got three children, the oldest of whom has just left home, loves travelling and changing her hair colour; a sport-obsessed teenage son with a crazy sense of humour; and a younger one who is fiercely stubborn (no idea where she gets that from), with a love of all things creative and stationery (yes, as in paper and pens, not things that are still – that would be weird). Along with some bunnies, and a cat with dementia, we live in a lovely, arty and slightly crazy town on the edge of the South Downs in Sussex.

In many ways, being a ministry mum is no different from any other household with working parents. This is, after all, the twenty-first century and it's not that unusual to be a working family. Yet, me becoming a vicar has added a certain dimension to our lives that we hadn't envisaged – a patriarchal one.

Early on in my ordained life, I was told by a well-meaning colleague, 'I think it's impossible to do what you are trying to do' in response to a particularly busy week that I was having – the seeming implication behind it being, I could not possibly be a wife and mum *and* a minister all at the same time. Though my feminist spidy-senses were tingling, I wasn't all that surprised. There are still a fair few male-dominated attitudes across the Church and an inability to see things from a different viewpoint, largely based on a model of working that has male ministers with their female wives doing everything at home.

When I was ordained, there was only one other female priest in my diocese with younger kids, working in full-time stipendiary ministry (six days a week for the Church). Ministry life is hugely rewarding, welcoming the joyous reality of a vast and varied extended family, but the systems and structures to support mums in ministry are often sadly lacking.

That comment from my colleague, among countless others, has prompted me to write about the life of a ministry mum on many occasions and I want to say to anyone reading that this is a book about the *possible*. There *is* a place for ministry mums in the Church and there *are* ways to make it work for you. I am a minister, a wife and a mum; I'm doing the stuff and I am just one of many. I'm not saying it isn't hard work sometimes (OK, a lot of the time) and that there aren't days when I want to jack it all in (there are plenty), nor am I denying that there are occasions when my kids get beans on toast for tea or they go to school in grubby uniforms because the washing basket is overflowing; but being a minister and a mum are both the most rewarding things I have ever done. I love my job, I love the Church and I am convinced that God has called me to it, *alongside* being a wife and a parent. Not as well as, but alongside. Perhaps you feel the same?

However, as I have found for myself, it can be difficult to find role models or good guidance on how to balance it all, stay sane and still love Jesus. At times, ministry mum life has felt lonely and isolating, but, thankfully, investigations led me to one place that has consistently helped: a wonderful supportive group of ministry mums online. I've often thought that everyone should have a community like that to turn to and so this book has largely been born out of a desire to help and support others in this way and to counteract some of the negative rubbish that women in ministry hear, of which, believe me, there is plenty.

'Impossible' you say? Well, don't we believe in a God of the impossible?! (Luke 1.37, in case you were wondering.) Pierre Teilhard de Chardin (nineteenth-century French philosopher and Jesuit priest) is quoted as saying, 'It is our duty as men and women to proceed as though the limits of our abilities do not exist.' None of this is really about *our* abilities, is it? It's about all that God does *through* us and with the gifts and abilities God has given us. I am so thankful for that because, as many working parents will know, sometimes the reality is, we feel we suck at it all. People often say things to me like, 'I don't know how you do it' and the answer is, *I* don't. Somehow, and by some miracle, God takes my feisty ineptitude, my yelling at my kids when I step on an abandoned Lego brick, my irritation with certain members of church meetings and pours on a shedload of grace, because God knows I need it and, well, somehow it all just happens.

I hope this book offers you a balanced view of the reality of being a mum working in ministry while avoiding stereotypes. One of my pet hates is going to women's ministry events where the sole topic of conversation is the best place to buy clerical wear for women. Personally, I'd rather we focus on ministry, theology and growing as leaders, but we're all different. Some of us like sparkly things and heels, others like a good sensible boot (or, in my case, both); some of us like doing messy crafts with our kids, others leave that to the child-minder; some of us like nothing better than an afternoon baking, while others prefer to peruse the confectionary display at our local bakers; so I hope you will join me in celebrating *all* women in ministry, even in our differences. However, I should probably say, if you want a book about what women should wear with a dog collar, quick-and-easy recipes or how to iron a shirt in 30 seconds, well, you ain't going to find it here!

Everyone's reality will be different and so I'm delighted to include some stories from fellow ministry mums, sharing their own experiences. What I hope you will find is helpful and practical ideas, support and encouragement. There will undoubtedly be things I've missed and for that I can only apologise. I write from the perspective of being married to my husband and, although I did spend a few years as a single mum with my eldest daughter, I have not managed ministry as a single parent (if you do, you are officially amazing); nor do I understand how it is to minister as an LGBT parent or to be in a self-supporting role and, while I touch on these and other areas, please forgive any omissions or errors.

You might be reading this as a church leader, needing some support; or maybe you're at a place of wondering whether you will actually finish tomorrow's sermon because you have to get to school sports day first, after visiting a sick church member, buying biscuits for the elders' meeting and checking the lead on the church roof hasn't been nicked again. Perhaps you're wondering how long you can continue. Maybe you're a young woman sensing a calling to ministry, but unsure if there is a place for you among the dusty minds of male-dominated church leadership. Maybe you are a working dad with a ministry wife, trying to balance it all as much as she is, or maybe you are just my mum (hey, Mum!) Whatever the reason, I hope that some of what you read here might be useful for *your* situation, that you will be encouraged, inspired and, maybe along the way, have a laugh at this crazy woman trying to be a vicar, wife and mum all at the same time. Many of us in the Church are striving to break the mould, seeking to find new ways of doing ministry as a mum and creating unique moulds for each of us. I pray that you too might seek to break the stereotypes you come up against, learn to flourish and thrive as a ministry mum and encourage others to do the same.

Authenticity is the daily practice
of letting go of who we think
we're supposed to be and
embracing who we are.

(BRENÉ BROWN, 2018)

1

Unmumsy and unvicary

HANGING ON TO YOUR IDENTITY
BY YOUR FINGERNAILS

Denial, anger, bargaining, depression, acceptance; the 'five stages of grief' are well known. The 'Jules accepting a call to ministry' model, however, was an all-new adventure. It went a little like this: denial, hysteria, defeat. The denial phase saw me spending, not weeks but *months*, ignoring everything about the call and not even admitting it to my husband. The hysteria phase came later and involved a lot of soul-searching, some wine (perhaps more than 'some'), tears (a lot) and some snot (basically I was a mess). Eventually (and thank God!), I reached the stage of defeat, accepting that this was actually happening; God was calling *me* to ministry. I'm not sure where you are in your own ministry journey, whether you're just sensing a call for the first time or, perhaps, considering a new role, but the more I have chatted to ministers and mothers, the more I am convinced that this wrestle and confusion is one hundred per cent normal. What's more, as I look back to the start of my own journey, I see that at the root of all my wrestling lay one key theme: identity.

I know – 'identity' is a bit of a buzzword these days, encouraging us to step into and be all that God has made us to be. 'Find your identity in Christ' or 'Love yourself as God created you' are phrases I imagine many of us have heard over and over, but it's not that simple, is it? Issues of identity and the search for who we are begin earlier than many of us can remember.

When I was a kid, I lusted after my best friend's beautiful hair: thick, blonde and shiny. It was everything mine wasn't, as mine was short, unruly in its curliness and, ultimate crime, ginger. I loved the glamour of her swishy hair and all that it represented to me, along with her cute 'Tammy Girl' wardrobe and contraband eye shadow; she was the person I thought I wanted to be. By 13, my identity envy was focused on my new best friend's 'Dash' tracksuit (my supermarket version not cutting it *at all*) and, by age 17, the Dash lust had been replaced by a rather different desire for dreadlocks and piercings, this time emulating my art college mates' 'alternative' ways. For me growing up, shaping my identity was all about fitting in, being accepted and liked. Although this is no longer my desire – self-confidence reminding me that I was born to stand out – moulds and stereotypes continue to plague the role of 'minister' and 'mum'. Indeed, a large part of my struggle to step into my calling to ministry was feeling that I didn't 'fit in' to others' expectations – and, indeed, my own expectation – of what a minister *should* be.

Who should you be?

'You really are a breath of fresh air,' remarked one congregation member who had approached me immediately after leading a Sunday service. I smiled. In a church with three locations and six Sunday services, conversation with parishioners is often short as I dash between them, but, nonetheless, hugely necessary. This particular morning, I had a bit more time than normal to chat over coffee and so found myself wondering about her comment. As well-meaning as this statement was and as nice as it was to hear, implicit in it is: you're different, you're not what we're used to and you're not what we expected. Here it was meant in a positive way, that I am bringing something to the church that is needed, something 'other', something missing, perhaps, and I know it's a sentiment other female ministers have faced too, but one which has caused me to question my unique identity in the role.

When I became a mum for the first time, one of the first things I did was read up on it all. I had no idea what I was getting myself into and, as a single parent at the time, I found treading this pathway alone quite scary. Some of the books I read were helpful, giving me the basic facts – which were pretty terrifying. Others were really unhelpful – as was the advice to watch someone else's birth video. If you're pregnant for the first time, just don't – *what the actual . . . ?* The best books I read were simply very honest, making it all seem personal, not facts and percentiles, weights and sizes, but actual questions and thoughts from an *actual pregnant woman*. Perhaps that's why 'real mum'-type books are so popular now, because they are exactly that: *real*. They make us feel that, however we parent, however hard we find it, it's OK, because there are other mums out there right now, screaming at the wall or dreaming of a neat gin in a darkened room. The fact is, however, that the popularity of real *ministry* mum books is lagging far behind – this may even be one of the first! This means that, instead of having many real accounts and role models in ministry to help us in the juggle and the struggle, we are still left to navigate many 'oughts' and 'musts' and 'shoulds'.

God made us all different

When I first felt God's call to ministry, I remember thinking: why would God want someone like me to be a minister? Someone with a misspent youth, a ranty tendency, with piercings and tattoos to boot? Plagued by the stereotypes we're so often surrounded with, I felt that I wasn't really a 'typical' mum and I definitely would not make your average vicar! If I'm honest, since accepting the call to ministry, part of me has quite liked that I don't really fit those labels – there's something a bit rebellious about it – but at the time, I certainly felt a reluctance to admit what God was asking of me. The biggest, perhaps sole, reason for this was that I was trying to step into a picture of identity which was not mine. But God just turned up the volume, using increasingly interesting ways to show me s/he meant business, the final straw being a visit from (and I kid you not) a double-glazing salesman, who told me, in no uncertain terms, 'If God is calling you to something, you just have to obey it.' No new fascias or windows, just that – a whole sales pitch about calling!

God was reminding me, as God needs to remind me again and again, that we are all unique. In Psalm 139, the psalmist describes God knowing him intimately, even before he was born, intricately woven together in God's sight, and I believe God creates us all different deliberately, perhaps so that, *together*, we display all the vast characteristics of God.

Many of you reading this will have been to some form of ministerial training college. For me, this meant three years of mixing with a variety of potential ministers, all from vastly different backgrounds, styles of churchmanship and, in some cases, denominations. This brought healthy debate (though sometimes challenging!) as we learned from each other as much as our tutors what it meant to seek God, worship God and understand God from each other's perspectives.

As ministers, we all share the gospel in different ways and, as mothers, we parent in different ways. If God has made us all different, then surely s/he has given us all something to offer in that difference? God does not want us to be what my bishop referred to at our pre-ordination retreat as 'clerical cardboard cut-outs'. We are individuals, called as we are. If God has made us unique in our differences, in our gifts and talents, then it makes sense that people meet with God in different ways. Isn't that part of the beauty of being God's creation? I think that's why God calls such a diversity of people to ministry. Now I know using the word 'diversity' is tricky here, especially coming from one who ministers in the Church of England, but the whole Church *is* becoming more diverse. It might be a slow and steady change, but it's there and it is making a difference. When we minister in our own style, we help to make that change, whether that's because we are women or mums or because we bring something of our own unique self.

Perhaps we all have the capacity to be 'a breath of fresh air' wherever we minister. I wonder how many of us have forgotten how unique we are. How many of us are trying to fit into someone else's identity – as a minister or as a mother? I love Brené Brown's wisdom, quoted at the start of this chapter, that to be authentic we need to embrace who we are, rather than who we think we are *supposed* to be. I know that, for me, I've had times when I've found myself looking at how others parent and tried to emulate them and I've tried to minister how others do as well. Preaching is a classic example of this, such as when I find myself in an Evangelical church, where the classic 'four points beginning with "P" sermon' is a staple, but it is not one that comes naturally to me. My preaching style was described by my then training incumbent (a fan of the four-points approach) as a 'magical mystery tour'! At times I've found trying to fit into others' styles incredibly hard work and completely draining. It's good to have role models and seek advice from others, but both ministry and motherhood are deeply personal experiences and I firmly believe that if we seek to do them both with authenticity, as the people God has made us to be, we will not just survive, but thrive. The reality of life as a working mum in the Church is that it can be messy and chaotic a lot of the time, but we need our unique voices to tell our unique stories against a rather white, male-dominated background in the Church today. As we discern our own way as ministry mums, we can be a voice to each other, to encourage and to build up, but also to the wider Church, to show the different gifts and talents that we have to offer, enabling a fuller and perhaps more balanced picture of church leadership to be seen.

All of us, whoever we are and whatever we do, have a calling from God to be and to do – that's the best definition of the word 'vocation' that I've come across. And it strikes me that we can't really embrace the *doing* of whatever it is we are called to without understanding the *being* first. What's more, we can't break the mould of all that's gone before unless we have a pretty firm understanding of who God has called us to be.

Who are you, actually?

Before we put on the roles of pastor, vicar, youth minister, mum, priest, elder, wife, partner or whatever it might be for you, we need to ask ourselves, 'Who am I? And who has God made me to be?' These are questions that, I suspect, many of us ask ourselves often, especially when we go through big changes in life. These things can cause us to question not just our identity but also our place and purpose. This *can* be a good thing, helping us to reassess where we are and where we want to be, but it can also bring confusion, anxiety, more questions and a lack of decision-making.

Before reading on, why not take a few minutes to pray and ask God how you were created? Note down some thoughts about who you are. What are your key characteristics? What are your gifts and talents? What are the things you love to do? What makes you laugh? What is your favourite part of your job? What do you love to do with your kids? Perhaps in doing so, you might see a picture of yourself that you had forgotten or never realised. Perhaps it might be a step in embracing who you are or just a gentle reminder of the person God made you to be and the identity that you, and you alone, have.

Moses' story

Understanding my 'identity is in God', to me, means seeking to be the truest or most accurate version of who God has made me to be. When Moses asks how he should explain who God is to the Israelites, God simply replies, 'I AM WHO I AM' (Exodus 3.14). Wouldn't it be amazing to have that same confidence in ourselves and our identity? We should – we are, after all, made in God's image, but easier said than done, right? I love the story of Moses, not only for this assurance of who God is but also for the reminder that God uses messy, ordinary people just like us, because, let's face it, Moses can be a bit of a dork sometimes. Take the burning bush, for example, in Exodus 3. There's Moses, a shepherd at that point, in the wilderness with his father-in-law's flock and, all of a sudden, there's a voice speaking to him out of a bush. To his credit, he clearly gets that this is the voice of God. God explains his mission to free the Israelites from slavery and adds, 'Hey Moses, you are the one I'm going to use.' What does Moses do? He uses every excuse he can think of for why he can't do it. Then, as if a bush that talks isn't enough, God shows him three pretty miraculous signs, yet still Moses is like, 'Oh, please send someone else.' Understandably, God gets a bit narked (theological point: does God get narked?) and agrees to send Aaron with him.

When God called Moses, he was just an ordinary guy with an ordinary life. When he needed a bit of reassurance, the first thing God did was to use what he already had. God asked him what he had in his hand (Exodus 4.2). 'A staff,' Moses replied – the very thing he already knew how to use in his work as a shepherd. In a way, it was an outward sign of who he was, his status in life. Then God asked him to put his hand in his cloak before using that too as a sign – his own hand, a part of his body used for so many different actions, but just a part of him, of who he was. Filled with God's power, these two simple things performed signs and wonders for the glory of God. This gives us such a powerful message about how God calls us as ministers – right where we are at, in the middle of our lives, surrounded by what we have and what we inhabit.

When I first became a Christian, it was in the middle of the building site that our home was at the time. I had just come in from work, my small children were running around, there was noise, mess and disorder and it was into *this* that God said, now is the time, come to me, make your choice. This has stuck with me, that God *is* right in the middle of our mess, within our lives; not alongside them or separate from them, but right in the heart of it all.

The other thing that we might find helpful about our dorky friend Moses is that, despite seeing God do those amazing signs, he still got things wrong, like the time he bashed the rock instead of speaking to it or threw down the stone tablets in anger and had to trek back up the mountain to get some more (grumpy teenager, anyone?!) He gives me hope in both parenting and ministry. It's OK that I am continually unmumsy and a bit of a rubbish minister sometimes, because I'm not supposed to be perfect and God uses us despite our imperfections or, perhaps, even *because* of them. I know that I have looked back to my misspent past and wondered why God didn't bring me out of it sooner, but now I see that nothing is wasted. The fact that I feel comfortable around those living on our streets or struggling with addiction issues is only because of my own time spent in a darker place. The fact that I get a bit too angry or frustrated sometimes, God simply channels into passion and vision to see change where there is injustice. Even my love of red wine has meant some wonderful and deep conversations about faith have happened in the most unusual of places. If God can take Moses and his hesitancy, lack of confidence and impatience and use him in such dramatic ways, don't you think God can use you in your flawed identity too?

What's in your hands?

Just like Moses, God calls us in who we are and what we have. Moses had a staff at his burning bush moment; I had a chocolate fountain. The idea of what is in our hands, whatever it is, is a helpful picture for us to think about *how* God has called us. How might God be asking you to use the things in your hands for his glory? If it's a cuppa, maybe you could minister to people over coffee and cake. If it's a nappy – OK, let's not get too literal with this one – but it could be in the local baby group that you find a great place to minister. Has God made you the kind of person who loves sport or walking or live music? How might God use any of those things? I've heard of chaplains, for example, in lots of varied places: the arts sector, Goodwood Revival and beer festivals for a start. Many ministers also have paid jobs in secular employment and feel as much called to that as they are to unpaid ministry. Ministry is not one size fits all and there are so many ways that God uses who we are – our passions, our skills, our life experiences and our callings.

If you're reading this and you are both in ministry and a mother – or thinking of taking a step into either – it follows that ministry and motherhood sit *within* your identity, not over it. I personally refer to motherhood as a vocation, as much as ministry is. Not in the way that some more conservative commentators might use 'motherhood is a calling' to define women's place in the home, but more that neither role is one you can stop 'being' and you are usually 'doing' it as well. Both ministry and motherhood are things that can take up every fibre of our being. Both require much personal input – emotionally, physically and spiritually – and they both focus on pastoral care, teaching, humility and nurturing. I think we need to recognise and revel in the joint callings within our identity, even when that is messy and chaotic. It is in such tension that we might find it easier to work out what ministry motherhood looks like for each of us as individuals.

Sarah Mullally, Bishop of London, was interviewed by *Stylist* magazine in 2018 about women in senior roles in the Church and said this, speaking right into the issue of identity:

> As women I think we need to ask: OK, what skills do I bring? What gifts do I bring and therefore how do I inhabit this role differently? It's vital to not try and pretend to be anybody else because, actually, that's when we fail. When we are asked or appointed to a role it is because they're asking us to bring what we're good at and the skills that we've got.

A few weeks back, I experienced someone leading worship, singing, with her six-week-old baby strapped to her front. It was one of the most beautiful things I have ever seen. She was truly and unashamedly being who God had made her to be – using her God-given voice to help people experience the presence of God *and* nurturing her baby, within her God-given role of being a mother. She could have taken more time away from worship after having her baby, she could have let her husband look after her daughter while she sang, but she didn't because, in that moment, she seemed totally confident in who she is and, as a result, I felt she radiated God's love in that place. I am reminded of Mary's song (The Magnificat, Luke 1.46–55), as she worshipped God after the angel's message to her that she would carry God's Son, her soul completely glorifying the Lord and rejoicing in God her Saviour.

I know other clergy mums (and dads) who have presided at the Eucharist with a baby on their hip, served Communion with a snotty toddler at their side or swept up a little one into their arms while preaching, and no one has died. Ministry is not like most other jobs; our children are often with us and that brings a richness to our roles which can be beneficial to us, our congregations and them. But, as brilliant as this is, it isn't always going to be neat and tidy.

Stories that we now regale with humour were, at the time, often awkward, embarrassing and, in some cases, downright painful – like the time the lead was pulled from a keyboard mid-hymn by a wandering toddler or the time an altar cloth was pulled off, lit candles and all, by another ministry mum's child. A fellow clergy mum's five-year-old was sick all down her as she was leading a service; and another's nine-year-old raised a loud objection to the banns of marriage in front of a full church! One ministry mum even had to navigate giving the Palm Sunday sermon while two of her children had a full-blown fist fight at the front of the church. I think my personal favourite comes from a vicar in Kent, whose baby son had a habit of pooing almost every time he was in church and, in the starring role of Jesus in the children's church Nativity play, he caused Mary to look up in the middle of the play, smile and announce loudly to one and all that baby Jesus had farted!

Holding together the dual callings of motherhood and ministry, at the same time as standing firm in the fullness of who God made us to be as individuals, is worth the fight. In her book *The Gifts of Imperfection*, Brené Brown talks deeply about authenticity, suggesting, to truly embrace who we are, we need to believe that *we are enough*. Many of us preach week in and week out that Jesus loves each of us so much he died for us, his love for us is totally unconditional and we are created in the image of God, yet so often we find it hard to fully embrace this for ourselves. A fellow minister reminded me recently that we should preach the gospel to ourselves every morning. I don't know about you but, for me, I need to continually remind myself that I really don't need whatever today's metaphorical swishy blonde hair or posh tracksuit lustings might be; I actually am enough as I am.

Caroline's story

Revd Caroline Beckett is a vicar in Essex and mum to two teenagers. Her background encompasses a vast range of churches, from Pentecostal, Charismatic renewal, Methodist and Anglo-Catholic to her current church, which is traditional in style with Evangelical elements, and she's married to a Baptist Mennonite. She has done ministry as a vicar's wife, while grieving as a widow, as a single mum, while dating, and now, married again, as a newly constituted family. She also has amazingly colourful dreadlocks and a sort of hippie–goth fusion look going on.

❜I realised quite early on in ministry that I had a choice to be "completely me", which might make some people uncomfortable; or to be half me and half another, perhaps more acceptable, version of me; or just to conform. In fact, there was a stage when I was first a vicar's wife that I did try to conform, largely to make it easier for my husband to fit in. I dressed in Laura Ashley with the "ladies who lunched" and then, outside church, we'd go out, authentically ourselves, in our goth gear. There was one fateful occasion when we went out to a gig in Camden. I was dressed in thigh-high boots and a leather corset, when I saw some of our parishioners approaching along the road. In true movie fashion, I pushed my husband against the wall and kissed him passionately until they had passed us. He surfaced, wondering what had just happened, but it saved us from a very difficult conversation!

This stage of life made me realise that we were trying to be who we weren't and we were both miserable. God didn't call me to be miserable and trying to be someone I was not was having that effect. One thing I've realised is that people tend to be less forgiving of diversity when you are female – it's as if being female is diverse enough. I'm a female vicar and anything more than that just makes me seem odd and can give people purchase for negativity.

However, I do have a sense of humour about how I am sometimes received. I am quite well-spoken and so I don't really look how people expect me to, nor do I speak in the way my appearance suggests I would, which can make for an interesting first meeting. If someone has only spoken to me on the phone, the reactions can be quite funny.

As a parent, I want my kids to have a healthy and robust spirituality and that can easily be affected both by my own behaviour and by how they see my church treats me. They know that I am comfortable in who I am, but they also know that I hold the tension carefully. They will clock when I have an important meeting as they will ask why I look so normal! But my being faithful to who I am has made it easier for my kids to own their own identity too. My daughter is mostly goth, while my son tends to go for a steampunk look and it went down really well at my investiture in my current church. This congregation is so accepting of who we all are and, in fact, one parishioner gave my son an old top hat that he thought would go well with his look. I'm also aware, though, that I don't want to get in the way of people encountering God. My identity is not just in how I dress but also in my role as a servant of God. As ministers, we often need to go into others' territory, especially when they are vulnerable or in need, and we need to learn the art of disappearing, to be a window and not a portrait. Each time I put on my stole, my prayer is that God may increase and I decrease, that his identity would be what people see through me.**'**

Sometimes the fact that there is nothing about you that makes you the right person to do something is exactly what God is looking for.

(NADIA BOLZ-WEBER, 2015)

2

Moulds and hammers

SMASHING THE WAY IT'S ALWAYS BEEN DONE

'So why do you want to be a priest, then?' The bishop questioned me with a steely eye during my pre-approval-for-training interview (to be fair, it might not have been steely, but it felt it at the time). My mind raced to find an acceptable answer. Like many people in ministry, I often get asked if it is something that I always wanted to do. The answer for me is 'No, *never.*'

My childhood dream was probably as far away as you could get – I wanted to be cabin crew. The feminist in me is rather ashamed to admit that I was drawn to the tall, glamorous British Caledonian 'air hostesses' (as they were then known), pictured in far-flung airports. They were like no women I knew and I wanted to join them in their mysterious, beautiful gang. In my defence, at that stage I had never left the UK and my parents, lovely though they are, were not what you'd call glam; I think my mum still has the same make-up bag with the same lipstick in that she had before she was married!

I struggled to answer the bishop's question in that interview, perhaps for the very same reason that I struggled to answer another question posed to me a couple of years later by a slightly drunken man hollering from the other side of the road, 'AW-RIGHT FAR-VER...!' As I walked across to him in my dog collar, I laughed questioningly, 'Father?!' He paused while considering this, then, looking pleased with himself, said, 'Sister?' I smiled as he went on, 'I mean, what should I call you?' 'I respond to most things, but my name is Jules,' I replied, opening up an interesting conversation, but one that left me reminded afresh of why I had so struggled to answer the bishop's simple question. Growing up, my own experience of vicars was that they were all blokes, grey and stuffy and, in my young eyes, old and boring (apart from one who used to come to church with his football scarf over his robes when Liverpool won – he was cool). Discerning my calling, I felt that there was only one shape of ministry and the Church was going to make me fit into it no matter what. Leaving my new drunken friend, I questioned again: what *does* the mould of a church minister look like in the twenty-first century? And what does it look like for those of us who are also mothers?

A reinforced mould

I know that I am not alone in finding the church leader mould a difficult one to step into; I find it's a regular conversation topic with those considering ministry. For many of us, across denominations, the role we are called to has been shaped by centuries of patriarchal leadership in the Church. Job descriptions describe a perfect person who will be available 24/7 at the drop of a cassock (on second thoughts, let's not think about dropping cassocks), with no thought for personal or family well-being; expectations of when hours should be worked are often based on 'that's the way we've always done it'; and senior leader roles are still often accommodated by men, many of whom live a traditional lifestyle with a wife at home who looks after the house and children, stocks up their sock drawer and buys their mum's birthday hydrangea each year (come on, I'm sure we all know one). The mould we see modelled to us is still largely white, male and middle class. In my time in church leadership, female colleagues have been few and far between – unless they are admin or support staff. At ministerial gatherings I am often the only woman and I regularly encounter surprise when people see me in the collar or meet me in person for the first time and discover that I am, in fact, a woman.

In many ways it *is* understandable that the system, structures and personnel still reflect this male history in large measure, as the wider

Church has existed for a very long time without significant female leaders. Dates vary but massive kudos to both the Salvation Army, which had female leaders from the very start in 1878, and Assemblies of God, which ordained women from its inception in 1914. Aside from these, there were a handful of female leaders ordained in the nineteenth century, largely to free churches, which were self-governing. In the Church of England, it was only in 1987 that women were first ordained deacons and in 1994 as priests (though, of course, this varies across the Anglican Communion); in the Methodist Church in the UK, women have been deacons since 1890, but only Presbyters since 1974; and for Baptists, again it varies, but in the UK, the first recognised female minister was in 1918.

Even in those denominations in which women have been accepted as leaders for some time, many of us still find ourselves arriving into church leadership feeling like the world has gone back 50 years, especially if you've had a job in the secular world prior to church work. My husband, who works for a large corporate organisation, finds some of the male-dominated ways of the Church questionable, arcane and definitely backward. We have some interesting chats about my 'employer'.

Add to all that a mould for Christian wives and mums that is still, in many quarters, rather traditional and it can feel like we're fighting a battle on all fronts. I have found that even where there is a greater acceptance of women who work, there are still underlying perceptions around the moulds of both motherhood and fatherhood. 'It must be so hard for you, preaching all morning and then heading home to cook lunch for the family too,' commented a churchgoer recently as I left the final service of the morning. I wasn't quite sure how to respond. I could have been painfully blunt: 'I have no intention of cooking the Sunday lunch when I've taken three services and overseen a deep pastoral conversation. I think I'll have a lie down instead.' Perhaps, alternatively, I could have smiled sweetly and muttered something about quick cook pasta. Other ministry mums and I have joked about the comments we've all received over the years, about our own mothering or lack of it or, indeed, over how marvellous our husbands are for taking on things at home that we all consider quite normal. The Sunday lunch question is a regular one or the question, 'But who will cook for your family if you have an evening meeting?' A friend was even told, 'Isn't your husband wonderful in the kitchen?', simply because he had unloaded the dishwasher! Then, of course, there's the old, 'Is your husband babysitting?' Well, no, actually, he's spending time WITH HIS OWN CHILDREN. One CofE canon even recounted how, early on in her clergy life, a church member commented, 'Isn't it wonderful your husband is *allowing* you to train?' . . . [silently shrieks].

Remoulding the mould

As frustrating as it may be, we cannot control what questions we are asked. We can, however, choose how to respond. A lot of the time I choose to laugh, because there are just too many to flag up. Perhaps that's a cop out and there are some who would say we should challenge all and any stereotypical views and comments. Certainly the constant drip of negative questioning and comments, while not an obvious 'enemy', can still be incredibly draining. In my experience it is usually, but not always, the older members of our congregations who make comments that we might find rude, derogatory, sexist, outdated or *insert your own adjective here*, but who often don't *mean* what they say to be offensive. I believe it's important for us all to find our own way, so try to decide where you personally draw the line for what is worth getting wound up over and what your response will be.

Feeling particularly bolshy one week, I responded to a comment made to me by preaching the following Sunday using only female examples in my sermon, and I deliberately used *a lot* of examples, with pictures! It felt validating when my colleague noted the following morning that people might have found it off-putting, giving me the perfect opening to highlight that this was probably what women felt every single week and to ask when was the last time he had used a female example in his sermon. As a result, we had a good and open conversation about how we address gender balance in our preaching. Sometimes helping others to see the lenses in their eyes is all we need to do to challenge the moulds we are surrounded by.

This was apparent recently when I was invited to attend a ministry conference that was open to both male and female leaders, at which the keynote speaker was someone well known for having a complementarian stance, whose theology meant that he did not support women in ministry and who was very public about it. I then discovered the entire line-up of speakers was male. My first reaction to this, which my husband can attest to, was explosive anger: how on earth did the organisers think it acceptable in this day and age to reinforce such a male ministry mould and, more, to expect women to come to it? *And breathe . . .*

Then I took a moment to actually ask myself that question – *why* did the organisers think this was OK? It occurred to me that they probably just hadn't considered it to be a problem. Putting aside for the moment the ministry mould which underpins that particular viewpoint, I thought about how I might challenge it. I could respond in anger (and, believe me, having the maturity to not send a ranty email is something I shall always pride myself on) or I could point out the problems. So, instead, I gently suggested the way this line-up might make female ministers feel, asked if there were any women in the organising group, added a few stats for female church leaders and highlighted that this could be a real opportunity for them to make a statement, pointing them to the Project 3:28 database of Christian female speakers. To their credit they responded with absolute grace, I felt heard and they agreed to find a female speaker for the bill. I'd like to say I deal with all the everyday sexism that I face with such calmness and dignity, but my colleagues would tell you it is utter BS.

There are, of course, plenty of positive stories from other ministry mums. Several ministers told me that they felt really validated and supported in their ministry regardless of their gender or mother-hood. One mum told me how positive her experience had been of residential training with kids – not only did she feel incredibly well supported by her college but she also noted how living in community was a hugely positive experience for her children.

In the URC, which has had female ministers for over a hundred years, the gender bias is often far less apparent and one URC minister shared with me how she had felt really well supported as a mother during assessment, training and the call process. She shared that her moderator and others supporting her had been really encouraging in thinking realistically about the needs of her wider family along-side training and ministry. As a result, she feels better equipped as a mother and minister to fulfil both callings, knowing that she is affirmed in both; and that ongoing and genuine support is available to her as she continues in ministry.

Remoulding Junia

Though female ministry role models are often outnumbered by male, they do exist and can be found – though some are harder to find than others. I was amazed, intrigued and wildly irritated all at the same time when I first read about Junia, a woman *and* an apostle mentioned in Romans 16 – yes, that's right, a *female* apostle named as such in the Bible. If you've never heard of her, I urge you to look her up; she deserves to be recognised and not, as did happen, written out of the history of empowered women because a few men remade her in a male mould. For centuries, no New Testament translation had Junia as anything *other than* a female name but, as Scot McKnight writes, a male mistransla-tion, made popular by Martin Luther, meant that for years Junia was seen as a man. In some translations, a small footnote suggested that hers could be a female name, but in later editions, it was removed entirely.

Writer of Romans, St Paul is often slated as being misogynistic and anti women but, despite some difficult passages in his letters,

I generally find him to be pretty *pro* women. Romans 16, where we read about the fated Junia, starts off by commending Phoebe (*clearly a woman*), a deacon (or minister). He goes on to mention Priscilla, whose name occurs *before* her husband's (almost unheard of), and who clearly ran a church together with him in their own home; Mary who worked hard; Tryphena and Tryphosa, women who worked hard in the Lord; Persis, another woman who worked very hard in the Lord; the mother of Rufus; and Julia, the sister of Nereus. Hardly sounds like a man who was not a fan of women, does it?

McKnight suggests that the reason Junia became known as a man was simply because it was inconceivable to later church scholars that an apostle could be a woman. Oh my! Inconceivable? Were our male scholars so insecure about female leaders that they had to remove them from history? Sadly, that is the kind of attitude women have had to deal with for centuries and, in some cases, found clever ways to manage it and challenge it. Historically, several female writers used pen names in order to get their work accepted – even J. K. Rowling (Joanne Rowling) was urged by her publishers to use a less gender-specific name for her work in case boys would not read it, which seems ludicrous given that the first Harry Potter book was only published just over twenty years ago (1997).

This cannot be what God intended. After all, when God created humanity, the Bible tells us:

Then God said, 'Let us make humankind in our image, according to our likeness . . . So God created humankind in his image, in the image of God he created them; male and female he created them. God blessed them, and God said to them, 'Be fruitful and multiply, and fill the earth and subdue it; and have dominion over the fish of the sea and over the birds of the air and over every living thing that moves upon the earth.'
(Genesis 1.26–28)

Humanity was created in the image of God, both male *and* female, and together given the responsibility to oversee the earth and all within it. That was God's original plan, male and female working together to manage creation, so why not God's Church too? Let's not forget the seed of women in church leadership was planted by Jesus himself, who shattered cultural thoughts about women and their place and who gave the first mandate to share the news of the risen Christ to a woman: Mary Magdalene.

Hillary Clinton, in her keynote speech for 'International Crisis Group' in 2012, said that 'Women are the largest untapped reservoir of talent in the world'. She said these words in relation to peace-making and women's influence in the communities around them, but noting how in leadership roles their influence might have a much greater impact. Women *are* using their talents all over the world; the problem is exactly as we found with Junia and J. K. Rowling, that the talents, skills or leadership qualities of women are often overlooked, simply because they don't fit the age-old, male mould.

Making your own mould

Many early female ministers found themselves trying to fit into a male mould in order to break new ground as the first women to take on such roles. It is only down to them fighting forward and making sacrifices that we can fill their shoes today. However, I believe that it is vital for us now, as women and mothers, to *continue* this work by finding our own moulds.

Today, working families in general are pretty standard. According to figures from the UK Office of National Statistics (Spring 2018), almost 60 per cent of households are working households (where all members aged 16 or over are employed). Working parents are such an integral part of the UK workforce that big businesses know, if they want to get the best out of employees with families, then they need to support them as parents as well as workers. 'Working

Families' (a UK work–life balance organisation for employers and parents) points out that, for most parents, family is their number one priority, so with working parents in the UK making up more than a third of the workforce, we need initiatives which will help them to balance work and family life *and* progress in their careers. Flexitime, job sharing, good maternity packages and shared parental leave all help parents to do their paid work, knowing that their employer will be supportive and understanding of other important demands on their time. In their recent 'Working Families Best Practice Awards', the top nominees included several large companies, banks and accountants and, perhaps surprisingly, the RAF – something you can read more about in RAF chaplain Ruth's story in Chapter 6.

In 2015, the Bible Society did some research on mums in full-time ministry. Encouragingly, a whopping 82 per cent of respondents said that they felt happy or satisfied in their work and it's a sentiment echoed in the research for this book. The colleagues I have spoken to who are truly thriving, not just surviving, are those who are working out what their own ministry mum mould looks like and not trying to fit into an outdated stereotype.

There are also those who have had cause to question their calling, felt a lack of support and faced opposition. One of the biggest fears I hear from young women exploring a call to ministry is how it will affect their family or any future family, and rightly so. The truth is, it can be a battle sometimes to put across our needs and concerns in a male-dominated system. One ordinand told me that, despite her request to be able to worship with her family during training, she was being made to do a three-year placement in a church with no provision for younger children. This seems a ridiculously short-sighted decision that has been made without any consideration of her motherhood and will probably affect her training and ministerial formation, as well as her family.

Just as the business world has learnt that it needs to look at different ways of working, there are those seeking to do so in the Church and there are many examples of women being encouraged to seek out what ministry looks like to them personally. Several women I've heard of have taken babies along to training weekends, clergy conferences or even ordination retreats – something that should not just be 'allowed' but encouraged.

As ministry mums, our moulds will almost certainly look different from those of women without children. I mean, getting up to lead an early morning prayer meeting after a night of vomiting children is not going to be fun, right? Lack of sleep might well factor in how you shape your ministry life, for example. In *The Unmumsy Mum,* Sarah Turner says that if sleep were a drug, she would lock herself in the bathroom and snort it! Sleep is such a simple thing, but actually lack of it can seriously challenge our sense of perspective on life.

One of the central things in moulding what your ministry should look like is, in fact, losing the *should* from this sentence. A phrase I've heard from American leadership writing is that we need to 'stop should-ing on ourselves'. I don't believe that ministry *should* look any particular way or have a prescribed pattern, and church leadership might take a different form depending on your denomination, your church and your role, but one vital area we can look at, which I believe is relevant to us all, is how many hours we work.

I have regularly come across the idea that full-time church leaders work 60+ hours a week. It's a figure bandied about with little question, so I did a brief (less than scientific) survey via social media asking fellow ministers how many hours they worked each week. I was staggered to find that over 65 per cent of full-time ministers surveyed work, on average, more than 50 hours a week, with over 25 per cent of them doing *more* than 60 hours. Yet the European Commission's rights for workers, set out in its 'Working Time Directive', require that weekly working hours should not exceed 48 hours on average (including overtime) and research shows that levels of productivity dip massively after 50 hours of work. Worse, if you work more than 55 hours a week, you are at increased risk of health conditions including stroke and heart disease. So, if this is the mould modelled to us, is it actually doing more harm than good?

I also found in my own research that, while there are increasing numbers of women in ministry, often women only take on part-time roles, enter ministry later in life when children are older or have partners who work part-time or not at all in order to manage the home. It's also worth noting that many female ministers are encouraged to undertake ministry on a self-supporting or voluntary basis, often working alongside paid work and/or family at home. While the ministerial hours might be less, coupled with everything else, self-supporting ministers can end up doing more hours' work overall than someone in full-time paid ministry.

I wonder if the deficit of full-time ministry mums is partly because the moulds of ministry we see model an unachievable or unattractive work–life balance. Is this potentially putting off younger women from entering ministry at all? I've got to be honest, much as I feel called to be a mum and a minister, I don't think it's realistic to work 60+ hours a week long term and not suffer the consequences. Inevitably there will be the odd week where it is unavoidable – a sick parishioner, the wedding season, a preacher cancels at the last minute – there are lots of reasons why some weeks are busier than others, but this should not be the norm. Let's not forget, as ministers we also have a responsibility to model to our congregations a good work–life balance within our own mould of ministry.

Pioneering a mould

Whatever our particular roles, we are all leading the way for our sisters to lead in the future. The Church as a whole sometimes feels like it has the turning circle of a slightly mouldy caravan (but with some nice retro curtains at the windows) and so can be incredibly slow to change. But we do have a hand on the steering wheel; there are plenty of others steering in the same direction, breaking down stereotypes, pushing forwards and seeking to shape moulds that work for all. The year I was priested (2017) was only the third year a bishop consecrated to our diocese ordained women; prior to that they shipped someone in from outside. That very first year, the bishop in question personally hand-delivered a rose plant to each of the women he was ordaining with a note saying, 'Sorry this has taken so long.' Thankfully he is not the only cheerleader; there are many others urging us on too.

Slowly, slowly, we are beginning to see ministry modelled in different ways. One of those who does is US Lutheran pastor and ministry mum, Nadia Bolz-Weber and, if I'm honest, I've got a bit of a girl-crush on her. As someone who is rampantly sweary and has a pre-pastorhood history of paganism and alcoholism, Bolz-Weber is perhaps not everyone's cup of tea, but she gives *me* a huge amount of hope, because she totally smashes the pastor mould. Refusing to conform, starting her own church and challenging age-old norms, in many ways she has made her own mould for a ministry in which she can thrive. She does so with painful honesty, accepting her own flaws with humility, but breaking down what she sees to be unjust or unworkable and with a feistiness that comes from an understanding of her own identity. Bolz-Weber gives me hope in a God of difference.

Right now, I know church leaders who are male, female, parents, childless, married, single, straight, gay, dreadlocked and tattooed, glamorous and preened, loud-mouthed, sweary, gentle, thoughtful, hysterically funny, not at all funny (if only they knew . . .), but God has a role and a place for them *all*. Each of them is being used to further the kingdom of God here on earth, so, whatever shape you are, there *is* a mould for you.

Made for this

'So why do you want to be a priest then?' Perhaps it is little wonder that the bishop's question, recalled at the start of this chapter, would prompt an array of complicated answers and complex feelings in me.

Yet, there are also times when the answer feels so very simple: this is what I was made for.

A few years back, I experienced having a 'sound portrait' from the group Epiphany. Seems strange, but, as I understand it, the musicians literally play what they feel God is saying, so it is a portrait of how God sees you, but in sound. Nothing planned, no score to follow, they just play from a place of prayer. It's almost impossible to describe, but in a few short minutes, I went through a range of thoughts and feelings, sensing things within the melodies, and then there was a moment when it felt like the music was literally flowing through my soul. In that moment, I knew exactly who God had made me to be and every fibre of my being was recognising its potential, its purpose, its true state. I didn't come away with a plan of action, knowing where God was going to take me or what ministry or family life was going to look like for the next ten years, I just knew that it was the shape of my life, one that would never fit into a different mould.

I look back now to that childhood dream of working in a place where I could jet off to far-flung corners of the world and wonder if there was something in the younger me that wanted the excitement of the unknown. I don't know, but I definitely find myself in a 'job' now where the unknown is a daily reality; where I am regularly flying (by the seat of my pants); doling out sustenance (of the Eucharistic kind) and dealing with duty free (forgiveness). If you've ever been in the place of exploring ministry, perhaps like me it's a mould you never thought you'd look at inhabiting. Perhaps it has become like a comfortable pair of jeans, but let's remind ourselves again, in the words of Nadia Bolz-Weber, that whatever challenges we may face, whatever battles we have to fight, 'sometimes the fact that there is nothing about you that makes you the right person to do something is exactly what God is looking for'.

Helen's story

Revd Canon Helen Cameron is Chair of the Northampton District of the Methodist Church and an Ecumenical Canon at Peterborough

Cathedral; she has been ordained since 1991. Helen is married to Iain, a GP, and they have three children, all now over twenty.

❝I made a commitment to Christ at the age of 11 and, surprisingly, felt the call to ministry at the same time – though I don't think I could have articulated it then, especially when the only people I'd seen ministering were chaps with white hair! However, my parents were lay preachers, so I started going out with them and was teaching and leading worship by age 13. At 16, I was given a "note to preach", doing my A levels during the week and preaching at weekends and I was accredited by age 18.

My journey was unusual from the start, so I suppose I was challenging the mould from an early age and in many ways that has been the hallmark of my ministry life. I'd only been ordained five years when I took my first maternity leave, being the first female minister in my circuit. I had to say to people, "It's OK, folks, don't panic, it's just like a sabbatical, but when I come back I won't have written a book but I'll have had a baby!"

As working parents, we believe that work is not about the accumulation of riches but the attitude of loving service, recognising we are *both* in public service. Understanding the importance of each other's work and not putting one above the other has been vital to making it work. My children have experienced us both working and have seen me exercise leadership in the Church, so they have grown up with a conscious understanding of equality in every way and could not imagine a world where one role was more important than the others.

Some combinations of jobs were, of course, harder than others for us to manage. Proposed flexible patterns of ministry by the Methodist Church, for example, did not quite match up with reality – part-time posts were often part-time pay with the expectation of working full-time hours and no housing provided. Early on I did some bits and bobs of teaching on pastoral theology and ethics for the Queen's Foundation, which, initially, was "putty-filling" for an all-male staff, and they later offered me a full-time job. The hours were more regular and worked well for us when the children were small, but the support of the college principal was also a key factor. Revd Dr Canon David Hewlett is deeply committed to building flourishing ministry for women and his contribution to my ministry made a huge difference, even when I took two maternity leaves in successive years! I sometimes taught lectures with a baby in a bassinet at the back of the room and have since found it an absolute joy to have a breastfeeding student in the classroom.

Sadly, there is prejudice in the Church and I still come across people who say, "Who's going to get his tea?" (meaning my husband), from time to time but, in the main, I've learnt which battles to fight. As chair of district, though, my experience of senior leadership has been largely positive; there is a firm commitment to make more female senior appointments in the Methodist Church and we've had three female presidents of the Conference in three years, which is really encouraging. When senior leadership includes good numbers of people who've been on maternity leave, struggled with childcare or understand the balance of ministry-mum life, then the system will change.

There are those who worry about deploying a woman with children, but there are others who see women with children as a gift of diversity and that's where we can best thrive in our own mould. Perhaps one of the most powerful things I've experienced is being a pregnant minister presiding at Communion – giving the life-sustaining bread into people's hands, while also sustaining a life inside me. To be a life-bearer is a wonderful model of spiritual life, where we might ask: how do we make a world that is warm and sustaining for those we serve, for our families and for ourselves?

When women teach, preach and lead, even with babies on their hip, the pews rumble, the ground begins to shift, barriers are torn down and once-silenced mouths are opened. Other women are given the confidence that they are not only able but also called to use their gifts within the body of Christ.

(TARA BETH LEACH, 2017)

3

Becoming Mum

THE EARLY YEARS

Dragging a sleeping-toddler-laden buggy backwards up a flight of steps, while hoisting a screaming and hungry baby under one arm, my eyes desperately scanned the café for an empty seat in which I could feed the screamer. Of course, there were none and the queue was filled with the blue rinsers ordering their afternoon scones. Joining the queue and smiling sympathetically at those staring at the baby (now screaming at apoplectic decibel levels), my own tears were close to the surface. Finally, I sat down in relief, only to notice the breast milk clearly soaking through my top. Despair, though, quickly became heart-aching joy, seeing the tears of my youngest turn to gurgling satisfaction as I nurtured her.

While my baby years were before I was ordained, that same mix of wide-eyed innocence, urgency, fear and joy describe well my early years of ministry life. I imagine the sort of scene described above will be familiar to many of us and it's actually a pretty good metaphor for ministry life: the constant demands, the criticisms often unspoken in the background, the extremes of emotion, the needs of those around us, the feeding of others – and the clearing up of their mess – coupled with utter joy and fulfilment.

Not all of you reading this book will be ministering while pregnant or with babies in tow, but we have all experienced change and uncertainty. Whatever stage of parenthood you are at, some of the things covered here might strike a chord with you. More than that, if we are going to be an encouragement to each other, then understanding the needs of younger mothers, both practically and emotionally, can only be a bonus. After all, the journey to becoming a ministry mum has to start somewhere . . .

Family planning

You might be right at the start of the kids question; thinking and planning. Maybe there's something baking in your oven? Even a, 'Shhh, my partner doesn't know I'm reading this!' Having children is a biggie, isn't it? If you place yourself anywhere on this spectrum, then there may well be questions spinning around your, possibly hormone-overladen, brain. How will a baby change our lives? Will I be a good parent? Can I afford it? What will I do about work? How will I juggle it all? Are we ready for this? It's also amazing how questions that are perhaps less important in the grand scheme of things can completely take us over too.

Will I get stretch marks? Will my bump fit into the cassock? Will I breastfeed at church?

Perhaps the most important question is, 'When?' Family planning is rarely simple. I've lost count of the number of friends who have 'decided' that they are going to get pregnant at a certain time of year or stage in their career. While this is admirable in terms of organised planning, many of us will know just how unlikely it is for a pregnancy to happen just when we would like.

The journey to pregnancy, in itself, can so easily have an impact on our ministry life. When 'trying', the anxiety of the wait each month can be overwhelming. As I understand it, most doctors won't take seriously any concerns over not falling pregnant until you've been trying for six months to a year, which is a long time to continually process the hope and disappointment cycle, especially if you don't want people to know. The added societal pressure on young couples – 'When are we going to hear the patter of tiny feet, then?' – is unhelpful in the extreme, but nonetheless, it is a regular question posed to young women in particular. Then there are others of us whose partners just need to wink in their general direction and, bingo, blue line – perhaps unplanned, possibly inconvenient, sometimes a shock. For others too, there are further processes to go through: IVF, fostering, adoption, each bringing further uncertainty. Some of us don't need to imagine the pain of not being able to conceive or of grieving miscarriages, all the while baptising a steady stream of newborns – we have felt it for ourselves. 'How do I manage my emotions, my hormones or my raised and dashed hopes, in a public-facing role?' is a question some of us will need to consider.

For most of us, the answers to our questions won't be apparent until we are inhabiting them. Some of us might become instant earth mothers, wearing our babies every second of the day and realising that this is our true life calling and we can't possibly leave their side ever again. Others can't wait to get back to the gym/book club/workplace for some adult stimulation. So it's almost impossible to say how you will feel about going back to work after maternity leave until your little one arrives. We're all unique, we all parent differently and we all have different life circumstances to consider, but even with some spontaneity it's unlikely that the metaphorical stork will arrive overnight with no warning at all. To some extent there is time to think, imagine, pray and plan for the baby years.

Maternity mayhem

Maternity leave stories in the Church can be alarming, with some ministry mums still finding that they are the first one in their area or diocese to have put the maternity policy into effect and, in more than one case I heard, even had to write the policy themselves! The Church is often a bit behind on all this, largely because, in many cases, they only had to start thinking about it relatively recently, meaning attitudes towards female ministers' pregnancies can be a bit unhelpful. Sadly, I've heard several stories of women being refused ordination, made to wait to start curacy or having to delay taking up a position due to getting pregnant at 'the wrong time'.

If it helps, it isn't just the Church. In 2016, the UK Equality and Human Rights Commission published a report that found three out of four mums had experienced negativity or discrimination in the workplace around pregnancy, maternity leave and when going back to work. So the thing to remember is to inform yourself, find out what you are entitled to, consider what you and your family need and, if necessary, fight for it.

Pregnancy during ministry training is a key time to watch out for maternity provision – ministry mums regularly fall through a gap here. You might not know, for example, that if you fall pregnant in the final year of theological training and your planned first post is therefore delayed, it often means you are not covered. Training for ministry does not in itself make you eligible for maternity pay, as it is not considered 'employment', even if there is a job at the end of it. A few mums also mentioned that, even though they were training alongside undertaking a role in a church, they were surprised to find out they weren't covered either. In addition, if you are in *paid* employment at the same time as training, you may also find added complications over maternity pay if you are planning to move into ministry and not return to that job.

If you are in any form of work at all or self-employed, even on a very low income, you might well be eligible for Statutory Maternity Pay or Maternity Allowance and there is a handy online calculator that can help you work it out on the Government's website (at gov.uk). Where SMP or Maternity Allowance are concerned, a week's work can make all the difference as to whether you are eligible or not, so, even if you aren't considering having children quite yet, do look into the policies and what you are entitled to. It's much better to know well in advance and make plans if you need to. Maternity rights will vary from person to person and across denominations, but at the very least it's worth finding someone in your area, circuit or diocese who's been through it already and then go and pick their brains.

The good news is that, increasingly, there are more church leaders who are seeking to lead the way on embracing motherhood in ministry. The Baptist Union, for example, has recently published a guide for churches and ministers who are facing maternity leave. The idea for the guide came from Baptist Minister Revd Ruth Moriarty, who was the first minister in her church to go on maternity leave and found that there was no standard policy for the Baptist Church. (This is due to the fact that individual churches can choose whether or not to affiliate to the Baptist Union rather than it being a prerequisite. Policies are therefore made at a local level.) Ruth gathered the experiences of other mothers in ministry and put together what she found out in her short guide, which is full of useful information, much of which would be beneficial across denominations. What's more it is available to download free from the Baptist Union's website.

In the Church of England, Canon Andy Griffiths, who coordinates training for new ministers in the Diocese of Chelmsford, has conducted a survey of curates who have taken maternity or paternity leave and their supervisors, which informs those considering maternity and paternity leave now. It is a refreshingly open, honest and encouraging document. One curate shared that her incumbent was determined to make maternity a plus for her *and* the parish, even if that meant him having to change his schedules to fit her needs – and this was done entirely successfully. Another minister noted that her bishop put her pastoral care above the impact her maternity leave might have professionally. With this kind of support and encouragement, I am certain that women will find it much easier to flourish in their roles as ministers and new mothers.

Back to work

Once your tiny bean is here (or not so tiny – one at over nine pounds here, ouch), then the changes and questions will probably continue.

Becoming a parent has been described in various ways, but I think *Man vs. Baby* dad, Matt Coyne, sums it up perfectly when he says in an interview with *Honest Mum* that the best way to prepare for your new arrival is by 'Emptying your bank account, smearing vomit on your shoulders and yellow shit under your fingernails and avoiding sleep until you think you might die . . .' As a ministry mum, in addition to all that you have to juggle Sunday services, cranky parishioners and possibly breastfeeding in a cassock!

Not everyone successfully manages breastfeeding or even wants to, so no soap box here, but for me, it was really important to be able to feed my babies as long as I wanted – even after three bouts of mastitis, shelling out on Savoy cabbage to ease the pain (does that really work for anyone?) and one trip to A&E after one of them puked up blood, which, it turned out, came from me, the little vampire. Even in those tough times, for me it was a beautiful part of my early experience as a mother, so if it's the same for you, then don't let ministry get in the way. Thankfully, almost all the ministry mums I spoke to about this have positive stories to tell. Hannah, for example, a young minister in Oxford, posted a lovely Facebook selfie of her in a cassock breastfeeding her son and received much online love and support from a wide variety of people. Increasingly, ministry mums are reporting taking their babies on training weekends and retreats, so that they can continue to feed them or bond with them in the early months, and several ministry mums told me they were supported in juggling their diaries so they could continue to feed their babies.

Just in case you do face any opposition, you might like to know that the law supports breastfeeding mothers. In the UK, for example, under health and safety, flexible working and discrimination laws, employers must legally meet their obligations to breastfeeding mums. In many European countries, there is a statutory right for paid breastfeeding breaks and, in the USA, there is a federal Break Time for Nursing Mothers law under the Fair Labor Standards Act (FLSA). These laws generally cover things like providing a space for breastfeeding mums to rest if they need to and a private, clean space (not a toilet) for those who want to express – though, to be fair, this might be tricky in an ancient church!

'When are you going back to work?' is a phrase that can appear on the horizon like a dangled carrot or loom at you like the onset of flu. By the time I got to my third child, it was definitely more carrot than flu. Coupled with the general messiness of babyhood and breast-feeding, added to parenting a toddler and a pre-teen, I just stopped bothering to get dressed. I lived in a whirl of 'comfortable fit' and basic Ts because not only were they comfy and I didn't care if they got covered in puke, or worse, but I could sleep in them too. I'm not even going to admit to how often (or infrequent) outfit changes were. I had gone from getting up each day, taming my wildly curly hair and dressing for work with purpose to this slovenly heap of elas-ticated sweatpants who just wiped bums and poured out milk on demand. I was not all that happy.

Now, don't get me wrong, I love being a mum and some of those early days are my favourite memories but, for my family, me going back to work was the right choice. Did I find it tough being away from my kids? Yes. Were there tears? Plenty. Was I knackered? Yes – still am – but it also felt like embracing who I was again. This was a new version of me, though – one who loved being a mum, but also one who relished time using my brain away from the endless nappies and bodily fluids.

Not all of us will have the luxury of a choice as to whether to work or not – perhaps for financial reasons, maybe you're in tied hous-ing or there are the complications of paid childcare. However, if you are in a position to choose, first, let me say, consider it well. Many mums of young children will know only too well why torturers use sleep deprivation – it is such an efficient tool. A tired, busy, over-filled mind is not conducive to being rational – and the hormones don't help either. It's hard to make big decisions when you are in the middle of big change and uncertainty, so take it gently.

If going back to full-time ministry after having a baby isn't going to work for you, that is OK; be kind to yourself. For me, choice is a big part of feminism. We have so many choices today that women who have gone before us didn't have, the most important being what is right for *you* and *your* family. We don't all have to work ourselves into the ground to prove the equality point, but if you *do* want to work full-time, then think about what it looks like for *you*. Perhaps it means a job change for you or your partner or a review of the hours you work or finding roles that are flexible. It would be great if job shares in ministry were more of a thing, but, at present, sadly, they are few and far between. In fact, in the Church of England, it is impossible to officially share an incumbent's role (that is, the vicar in charge of a church) as, under current church law, only one person can be licensed as an incumbent to a parish, so even in the few roles where job shares are in place, they are often not officially such.

Another question you might want to consider is the effect a different role or part-time role might have on your long-term ministry. One Methodist minister shared with me how people viewed her completely differently after she had children. She found the assumptions that went with her new parenthood status unfair, with a sense of her whole vocation being perceived to have changed, that she would be unable to undertake official roles because she now had small children and the idea that she had publicly made a choice to stop being a valuable member of the church with strategic skills to offer. It was as if her former vocation and skill set had been eradicated by parenthood. This minister was not asking for any preferential treatment, but simply to be treated with the same level of respect for her professional skill set as she had been before the children were born.

Thankfully, as highlighted earlier, there are churches and leaders seeking to support mums. Andy Griffiths notes that churches where ministry motherhood is embraced are 'the sort of church that will retain some of its most gifted ministers and present to our culture a genuinely attractive vision of multigenerational community'.

Childcare

Depending on the choices you make about work, you may need to consider childcare. Allowing someone else the privilege of looking after your children is not an easy task but, once again, there is gradually more and more choice, so decide what works well for you. Here is just a handful of options chosen by some ministry mums I have spoken with.

Nannies

Often not affordable on a stipend/minister's wage but works for some, especially if the minister has income from a partner or elsewhere or can nanny share with another local family. Nannies tend to give you more flexibility regarding hours, illness and are sometimes prepared to do other domestic jobs.

Au pairs

Usually much cheaper than a nanny, but you may need space for them to live. Often younger and inexperienced, meaning turnover can be high if they are on a gap year, for example.

Childminders

Accredited, inspected and trained, but cheaper than a nanny, they usually cover fixed hours, meaning you can plan in advance. Your child/ren might well mix with others the childminder also looks after.

Nurseries/daycare

Can offer longer hours, which is helpful for antisocial meetings, but you often have to travel to find one, which adds time to your day.

Family and friends

If you are lucky enough to have family nearby, who are willing to help sometimes, this can be a great way of making sure your children are looked after by those you know and trust. They are likely to be more flexible, but it may put strains on relationships.

Parishioners

Some say they couldn't live without support from their congregation; others avoid such help like the plague and feel it has opened them up to extra criticism of their parenting.

Teenagers and babysitters

Great for evening meetings, much cheaper than childminders and nannies by a mile, but generally much less experienced. (Ours is fab, just next door and lots of fun – love you, Ella!)

Bloom where you are planted

I know, 'bloom where you are planted' sounds like one of those inspirational graphics that is passed around on Facebook, but I believe it's what we need to do, regardless of the particular decisions we make in the early years. Essentially, this is the message God gives to the exiles from Jerusalem who found themselves in a new life in Babylon. Jeremiah 29, verse 11, tends to get quoted a lot: '"For I know the plans I have for you," declares the LORD, "plans to prosper you and not to harm you, plans to give you hope and a future"' (NIV). When we look at this verse in the context of the whole passage, it shows that we have a role in our future and it might not always be what it seems. God's word to the exiles, finding themselves in a strange new land is to:

> Build houses and live in them; plant gardens and eat what they produce. Take wives and have sons and daughters; take wives for your sons, and give your daughters in marriage, that they may bear sons and daughters; multiply there, and do not decrease. But seek the welfare of the city where I have sent you

into exile, and pray to the LORD on its behalf, for in its welfare
you will find your welfare.
(Jeremiah 29.5–7)

The word from God for the exiles is to embrace and bless where
God has put them. Taken from a place of safety and into a new and
unknown terrain, the temptation must surely have been to stick
together in family units, not to challenge the status quo, perhaps even
to put up with or join with local customs that were not their own.
In many ways, we might find a parallel with our lives as ministry
mums here. God's message to the exiles, and perhaps a lesson for us,
is essentially to bloom where they are planted – to embrace where
they have been put; to settle, to build, to forge ties and to pray for the
area. In doing so, God says *in its welfare you will find your welfare*. As
ministry mums, perhaps we could view our 'terrain' with the same
outlook? How can we seek the welfare of our own surroundings as
well as our own? These are the kinds of questions Andy Griffiths
and Tara Beth Leach (quoted earlier) are asking – not only how can
ministry mums thrive but also how can we enable those around us
to thrive by bringing who we are?

Revd Dr Emma Percy has written about this too in her book
What Clergy Do: Especially when it looks like nothing. She does so by
looking at the similarities between mothering and ministry, high-
lighting skills across both roles with the aim of helping people to be
better ministers. She notes, 'Mothers are organisers, carers, com-
forters and admonishers, providers of food, teachers, playmates,
sounding boards, sympathisers, storytellers and boundary setters.'
Embracing our roles as mothers, as well as ministers, and fighting for both of them from the outset is a wonderful witness to our
congregations. Far from being a hindrance to ministry or a loss of
strategic skills, motherhood can enhance it, bringing new skills to
the fore.

Jac's story

Revd Jac Parson is a Baptist minister in Sussex and mum to two daughters under five. She has been a minister for ten years, in different churches and locations, in both full-time and part-time roles. She's been through two maternity leaves and is currently working in a part-time role.

❝One of the most important things I've found since becoming a mum in ministry is to set boundaries and then stick to them. I've been through two maternity leaves and the second one has definitely been more positive. I learnt so much from the first one and made some changes, knowing what I was and wasn't prepared to do. Sometimes people expect you to give blood, but my family has to come first. It actually took us a long time to get pregnant; in fact I didn't think I was able to, so now, even more so, I don't want to spend every waking hour working: life's too short.

Even having learnt to put better boundaries in place, maternity leave was still hard because I live in the community and because I love my job. I decided I would continue to attend deacon's meetings throughout my maternity leave as they are not that often and I felt it important to still be there for them. I've also been available for questions that have come from the church, because I know they genuinely care about my opinion on things. I have found that sometimes we need to fight for what we need or want and it's important to do that; our job is also to model a good balance and we probably don't do it enough.

After having my first daughter, I decided to move to a part-time role. My husband works full-time on shifts and we ended up spending so much on our nanny, often more than I earned, and, coupled with the amount of time that I was spending away from my daughter, for us it felt like the right thing to do for now. I like the freedom that working part-time gives me. It isn't always easy – I usually do more than my hours – but it still works for us. I get to spend more time with my kids and feel less guilty about doing things other than work. Being a mother certainly makes you more efficient and productive, because you have to be!

One thing I love about being a ministry mum is knowing that I'm helping to break stereotypes and barriers. There are still a lot of unfair expectations of us, ludicrous even, especially for those of us who have husbands who work full-time too. I've had some great opportunities that I wouldn't have had if I weren't a young mum. Not long ago, I was asked into the local baby unit to celebrate Pancake Day because, I was told, 'You're not like any other minister'!

My current church is really supportive. I led a service recently with my baby daughter in my arms as the babysitter hadn't turned up and they were very understanding. Another time my toddler was sick at nursery and I had to pick her up and then juggle the schedule for that day around her. It meant hosting a deacons' meeting at home with her, now apparently fine and very lively, running around in the background, occasionally asking, 'Are you *still* talking?' Some people struggle to comprehend the concept that you can be in both roles, but in moments like these I find there are people who really do just get it. **)**

Trying to do it all and expecting
that it all can be done
exactly right is a recipe for
disappointment. Perfection
is the enemy.

(SHERYL SANDBERG, 2015)

4

Endless expectations

AND NOT GIVING IN TO THEM

The little phrase 'it's impossible' came back with a vengeance as I contemplated moving on from my curacy. In the Church of England, once you've finished training at college you go into curacy – a training post that usually lasts three to four years. You are fully qualified in name when you start, but the intention is that, by the end of it, you will also have enough practical experience not to need supervision or perhaps to go solo. As the end date loomed and I looked to 'What's next?', fear overcame me: *Can I really keep up with all these expectations?* The pressure to 'do it all' and to do it all perfectly, as Sheryl Sandberg highlights opposite, was huge.

Expectation – it's a word filled with such hope and yet so often leads to a big reality check. Take motherhood, for example. I can safely say that I do not know any parent whose expectations of parenthood are the same as the reality. Newly pregnant, I dreamt of staring lovingly into the eyes of my soon-to-arrive newborn, but in that I was projecting an expectation shaped by societal perfection, which blooms in airbrushed magazines. What I didn't see coming was the downright messiness, the smells and the pain – think detailed conversations about nappy contents, mashed Weetabix concreted to the kitchen floor (how does it do that?) and the inordinate pain of a barefoot Lego brick injury.

Ministry is another example of when our expectations might be slightly off-key. Entering into discerning a call to ministry, I found myself thinking about how I could serve those around me; marvelling that I was following in the footsteps of great church leaders;

reflecting on how it would be a privilege to walk alongside those in difficult circumstances; and expectant that it would be *entirely* fulfilling. The reality *is* all of those things, but it's also: serving those who are churlish; working with church leaders with whom I disagree profoundly and, actually, sometimes it means dealing with things like clearing dog poo from the church path, which is arguably rather less fulfilling. In fact, I recently asked a bunch of church leaders for things they had faced through ministry life that were not expected and the answers were vast and varied. They ranged from the downright sensible, like not knowing how to manage conflict (particularly with the organist – this was a common thread); to the sublimely ridiculous, like learning how to pluck and gut a pheasant (rural minsters can attest to this, I am sure); being unsure as to the correct response when one's cat drinks the bishop's water at a confirmation service (I really must find out more about how that happened) and wondering how to inter the ashes of a dead pet!

Cheap laughs?

The comedic aspects aside, countless female authors have highlighted the expectations of women in the workplace that men don't experience, so what expectations could we face as ministry mums? For me, they began during the selection for ministry process, where it was assumed every area of my life would be examined – a bit like having a smear test that goes on for rather too long, but you know it will be worthwhile in the end. Have I gone too far with that analogy? Sorry, let me explain . . . it was generally intrusive, quite painful and intimately exposing.

In different denominations this selection process varies, but I'd suggest, wherever you are, one worthwhile use of the discerning time would be to work out what expectations there might be of you. Ask those who are guiding you in the vocation process, seek out other ministry mums, do a placement, take time to think about how realistic those expectations are for you and your family – from training, all the way through to running a church, and everything in between. This really will help you to plan for the future, but will also help those who are supporting you in the process, or seeking to find you the best post, to know where you will fit best. Where I've seen initial posts face real challenges, or even fail, it's often where the church's and the new minister's expectations haven't matched up. Sadly, there are still sacks of patriarchal views and misunderstanding across the Church so seeking to manage these expectations might not be plain sailing. For example, it's not uncommon for women to be told not to get pregnant during training or first post; or that they should have their children *before* going into church leadership or, as a mum, the only route into ministry is the unpaid one. Such expectations are unfair, don't take into account any potential for the pain of not being able to have children and can be hugely damaging to those exploring a vocation. If you face any of these kinds of attitudes, please do seek support.

Once you are ordained, licensed or in post, the expectations can just keep rolling in. In 2015, *The Spectator* magazine referred to job ads in the *Church Times* as good for 'cheap laughs'. According to these ads, churches are largely seeking a minister who will be available 24/7; have a family who will take a full part in church life, but never be a drain on the minister; have all the skills of management and leadership, but never actually put them into practice; be under 30, but have the wisdom of Dumbledore; and be the best preacher ever, but never need time to prep a sermon. Add to that mix how you balance this level of expectation with being a parent and . . . well . . . One ministry mum, on being asked if the Church had realistic expectations of parents in ministry, simply replied, 'HAHAHAHAHAHA. Yeah, no.' Such expectations can be reinforced by congregations too. As one single ministry mum announced to her church the joy she felt because she would be adopting a child, the response from one member was that it was very unfair she hadn't told them in advance of her intention to become a mum.

On my good days I try to understand what is behind any expectations or negativity thrown at me; on the bad, not so much. A woman who shouted at me in front of half the church, 'Call yourself a minister? You are just selfish . . .' when I couldn't meet with her right that very minute, I later realised was dealing with a deep sense of hurt from a lifetime of unmet expectations. It can be helpful to remember that expectation is often about the person who has it, not necessarily those it is projected on to – and, in recognising that, we might be able to deal with the underlying issue rather than giving in to the expectation itself.

The (overly) familiar

Expectations can manifest themselves in very practical ways, especially as we live in an age of 24/7 communication, where we want the information we need *right now*. The bonus for us is we are able to shop online at midnight for a next-day delivery; the downside is that the same might be expected of us. A 7 a.m. phone call about a possible baptism from a local family or an 11 p.m. Saturday evening concern about the relevant hymn book for tomorrow can be your new normal if you so wish, but putting some boundaries in can help us, and our congregations, understand when expectations are OK and when they are not.

I have learnt to say that an 8 a.m. prayer meeting on a Saturday is not going to work for my family and to screen my phone calls on the basis that if it's urgent, the caller will leave a message. I no longer apologise for a delay in replying to someone's email, because, if I say sorry, I'm simply reinforcing an expectation that I should have done it sooner. I do know one minister who, on returning from holiday, can't face the ridiculous email mountain to climb, so, rather mischievously, deletes the whole lot in the belief that important ones will be sent again!

There's something about being in a public-facing role that can foster a feeling of people thinking they know us better than they do. This can lead to people stepping over the line of personal barriers without the slightest concern, whether it be a rather forward kiss from a loose acquaintance or intrusive questions about personal health. Social media breeds this overly familiar expectation also and, as contemporary church leaders, we cannot post without considering its impact. Keeping church profiles separate from your own can help, as can letting your children know that they do not have to accept online interaction from church members. I find that having online public profiles which keep family stuff to a bare minimum allows me to accept as many followers as I like and is extremely useful for networking. We then have a more private family Facebook page to use for keeping in touch personally.

Divine expectations

A woman I find hugely inspiring is Bethany Hamilton. She survived a shark attack at age 13 and absolutely smashed any expectations after the attack that she would never surf again by realising her dream of becoming a world-class surfer. Hamilton notes that when she's 'unstoppable' (the title of the documentary movie about her life), it's because she views herself, her situation and priorities not through fickle human assessment, but through *God's* eyes. I've been reminded, perhaps with alarming regularity, that God's expectations of us are usually far less demanding and much less judgemental than human ones. Indeed, the Bible regularly reminds us to aim to see things God's way. Paul writes in Romans 12.2 (MSG):

> Don't become so well-adjusted to your culture that you fit into it without even thinking. Instead, fix your attention on God. You'll be changed from the inside out. Readily recognise what he wants from you, and quickly respond to it. Unlike the culture around you, always dragging you down to its level of immaturity, God brings the best out of you, develops well-formed maturity in you.

It is so easy to get dragged into the expectations of others, but what does *God* expect of us? What is *God* asking us to do? Paul goes on in this chapter to talk about how we need to work together in harmony for the body to work. We are *all* members of that body – church leaders, congregations, families – and seeking to find a way to work together which works for everyone is key. When we focus on what God is asking of us, then it's much easier to see which expectations are from others rather than from God.

A little while back, over coffee and tears, I shared with a friend about the previous busy few weeks of ministry life. 'Saying no is not only OK, it's essential sometimes,' she told me firmly. She gently reminded me to focus on what God was asking of me, not those around me. A few days later, I got a funeral request from a colleague. Remembering her wise words, I replied that I couldn't take the funeral as I was already doing 8 a.m. pastoral visits just to fit them in. His expectation was: *make time.*

So, in a display of 'well-formed maturity', I threw a few toys about my office, had a good weep, then put the situation rather grumpily back into God's hands, suggesting in no uncertain terms that God would have to find me some kind of supernatural timing. I then dutifully emailed the funeral director to ask for the details. Minutes later, she replied, very apologetically, saying that the family didn't want me – a woman. Normally, this would have sent my feminist side ballistic, but that day, I literally laughed out loud in my office and rather smugly emailed my colleague the news. I do love God's sense of humour sometimes.

Family expectations

Focusing on God's expectations of us is not just about minis-try but about our families too. What are God's expectations of us within our families and how does that play out in what they expect of us?

I once told my husband (before we were married) that, despite loving my job and being a fiercely independent type, I was going to give it up and become a stay-at-home mum. It's fair to say that idea went right out the window and kudos to you if you are a stay-at-home mum; frankly, I think you are a saint. My husband would be quite justified in pointing out that our life together is not quite what *he* expected. When I run marriage preparation for couples now, one of the biggest things I talk through with them is communication. It's unrealistic to expect our view of marriage or parenthood – or, in fact, life in general – to stay the same from our teens and twenties throughout life and all it brings. If we can keep communicating with those closest to us about what our expectations of each other are, then we place ourselves in a much better position to live a peaceful and united life. It's the same with our children, as their expectations and needs will change as they grow. If we can allow our expectations to change with them, rather than making decisions based on what we think our boss, colleagues or congregations expect of us, then the chances are, we'll all feel more balanced and calm. As they get older, they are much better able to share their own expectations and I've certainly found that when our kids are given options and choices, rather than being told what, where and when, they really appreciate it – after all, some of the expectations we face are projected on to them too. Many of us will have experienced the expectation that the minister's children are public property, will attend everything and shall at all times be perfectly turned out, well behaved and able to engage in polite conversation from the age of about six months. They shall at no time fart on demand during the Good Friday walk of witness, throw litter on the floor of the church and refuse point blank to pick it up or send Snapchats while playing in the worship band. Those were not my children. OK – that last bit was a lie.

If you are living in a church house, the expectations of family members can be even greater. We need to ensure that our children can expect to live in a home, not just an extension of the parish office.

May I suggest changing the locks if any parishioner has a key? We now encourage our children not to answer the doorbell after one fateful occasion when my youngest daughter let someone in and led that person straight to me . . . as I was taking a moment to lie in the garden in my bikini. Not sure who was more embarrassed there. The child and I had words. There can often be a great pressure to keep up appearances, to conform to what a 'vicar's home' should look like. But, if we're honest, all these expectations don't just come from others; *we* usually pile them on ourselves too and in spades.

Women of valour

Sometimes the expectations that I place on myself weigh as much as those others have of me. The Proverbs 31 role model of a woman doesn't help either. So often painted in the perfect light, rather like those mum friends who give off a social media air of smug perfection, the Proverbs 31 woman, in my eyes, shamed me: doing good, getting up super early, providing for her family, running her own business, helping the poor and all done in such a good-natured way. She seemed to have achieved an ideal balance that I was never going to achieve. I mean, even just getting out of bed in the morning is a struggle. I'm hardly likely to be up before dawn just so I can cook breakfast for my hoard, as she might have done. In fact, my husband fits this Proverbs 31 mould far better than I, being one who can bound out of bed at the mere hint of birdsong, filled with joy and raring to go, while I want to whack him and his dawn exuberance over the head with the bedside lamp. I wonder how many of us have been taunted by that passage or had it quoted at us in an attempt to show us what to prioritise in our lives?

In reality, though, these verses mean so much more than being a good wife. When I became a Christian blogger, one of the first books I was pointed to was by Rachel Held Evans, a writer and blogger with vast biblical knowledge and a passion for standing up for the rejected and excluded. Her writing on Proverbs 31 in *A Year of Biblical Womanhood* (2012) had a great impact on me, and many other women. She writes, 'The Proverbs 31 woman is a star not because of what she does but how she does it—with valor. So do your thing . . . do it with valor.'

Rachel Held Evans gently and firmly takes apart the way Proverbs 31 has been mis-sold, reminding the reader that really it is about being an *Eshet Chayil* – a woman of valour. I am writing this now in the days after her untimely death and find myself moved all over again at the impact she has had on so many people's lives. She wrote about her conversations with her Jewish friend, Ahava, who revealed to her that the essence of the *Eshet Chayil* is not the ideal model of a woman, but the valour that is in her, which is present in each of us too. Far from being a passage labelling women, it was an honouring passage that is sung or recited each week by husbands to their wives at the Sabbath meal, an unearned blessing, given unconditionally. For Held Evans it became an encouragement to share with other women doing things with valour, just as she did in her own too-short life. In many ways, that early input in my Christian journey has led to the writing of this book, that it too might be an encouragement to all the women of valour who read it – a reminder that we are courageously stepping into all we are called to, that we are all *Eshet Chayil.*

For us as ministry mums, this woman of valour gives us an example of the heart behind all that we do. We minister and we mother with valour – with courage, spirit, boldness and nerve every single day. The juggle is real, but the foundations come from that same heart which we have already looked at: our identity in Christ and in forming our own God-shaped moulds.

Jesus Jenga

To repeat: the juggle is real. Even with firm boundaries around the expectations we take on and limiting them to those that God is asking of us, balancing family life and ministry can still feel precarious – a little like a game of Jenga. Do you ever feel like that? How many bricks can be added on before the tower teeters and you know that, in a moment, life could come crashing down around your ears? Living out your God-given identity, and making your own mould, can succeed or fail based on the fine-tuning of your own *Jesus Jenga Juggle*, so here's a couple of practical ideas to help us along the way.

First – a word of caution to those starting out. Revd Canon Rebecca Swyer, who works in my own diocese of Chichester and oversees curates, suggests that new ministers often end up doing too much due to the enthusiasm they bring to their new role, but that a key part of a first post is establishing a sustainable pattern of life and ministry, including prayer and keeping boundaries, which will work throughout their lives. Thomas Merton is often quoted as writing that 'Happiness is not a matter of intensity but of balance, order, rhythm and harmony'. In achieving such harmony (ha!) perhaps we need to give ourselves permission to try out a few different things.

Aside from prayer, communicating through a domestic summit has become perhaps the most important thing my husband and I do to keep the tower upright. A 'domestic summit' is simply an intentional time we put aside to discuss everything we need to for the week ahead (at its best, held within the local pub). An essential part of this is a joint diary; for us it's online so it's easily accessible from anywhere, but a calendar on the kitchen wall might work just as easily for you. Another idea I've heard of is the traffic light system, which simply looks at all the things that need to happen in a single week and labels them red, green and amber. Green for go – all this must happen so get going. Amber – wait, is there time? Is it clear to go ahead with any task or activity? Red – stop! Do you really need to do this right now? This idea is great if you find it hard to order or prioritise things. Bullet journaling is another one that's very popular right now and it can help to keep things in priority order.

Scheduling in regular family downtime has been vital for us. Friday evenings are a key time; we are all in together for a chilled-out evening. These evenings are non-negotiable except for absolute emergencies and, though we don't usually plan much, the kids know that it's a night set aside for family, even if we're not *doing* anything together. If you're a Proverbs-31-rise-before-dawn-morning-person (and blooming well done there if you are), then it might be that getting up earlier before the kids are awake can give you some space to get things done before they need attention. This is referred to as the 'magic hour' by parenting 'expert' Samantha Ettus, who suggests that it can allow you to get up and get dressed at a leisurely pace, answer emails and have a cuppa, all before the kids wake up (though my failed attempts at getting out of bed earlier than absolutely necessary point to the fact this is not magic for me!)

Though my own *Jesus Jenga Juggle* continues to fall and be fine-tuned afresh, I do find that, as time goes on, the expectations I have of myself have decreased and my ability to say no to other's expectations has increased. I still serve those who are churlish; I still spend time with those I find annoying; I still have necessary late nights; I still clear up the dog poo outside the church gate; but with each year that passes, I feel better able to focus on God's expectations rather than on anyone else's.

At the end of my curacy, I was offered the role of associate vicar in the same church. Reflecting on the previous three years and contemplating whether or not I could handle the expectations, I knew that trying to do it all or seeking perfection was not something I wanted to carry with me to this new post. I spent time talking with my husband and children about the role and how they felt about me taking it on. This meant I was then able to talk with the rector about the expectations of me and the family, shaping the role so that it could work for us all. As ministry mums, I believe that we can continue to model something new, challenging expectations and modelling different, perhaps more realistic, ones that enable us to thrive.

Katie's story

Revd Katie Tupling is a ministry mum in the Anglican Church. She spent 15 years in parish ministry before moving into a diocesan role as 'Disability Advisor and Lead Chaplain among Deaf People' in the Diocese of Oxford. She is the founder of Facebook group 'Clergy Mummies' and a founding member of 'Disability & Jesus', an organisation that seeks to provide a theology of disability from a personal perspective. Katie is married and has a primary school-age son.

'At the age of seven I rather precociously said to my mum one day, "I'm going to become a vicar", to which she replied distractedly, "Oh, that's nice." But, despite this early call, as I got older, I fought the sense of calling all I could and the fact that women could not be ordained at that stage just gave me the excuse I needed.

Many others had expectations of me; everyone seemed to know and expect me to take this step, even when I didn't. When I finally went to talk to my vicar, he told me, "It's about bloody time." Later, attending an ordination service, an archdeacon I didn't know came over to me during the peace and just said, "Your turn next." When I quizzed him via email, he simply said, "Sometimes you get a word and you just have to pass it on."

Of course, in those early days of women being ordained there were all sorts of excuses, from the fact that I was too young, that I couldn't possibly explore the calling so soon after getting married and, in some respects, due to my disability – I have cerebral palsy – and later due to becoming a parent.

I would say it's vital to really know yourself before entering ministry, especially if there is something else to consider, like disability or being a mum. Go off and do some personality tests, get counselling if you need it, unpack yourself and your life. If you have a disability, work it out in your voice, aside from the medical diagnosis you were given or your family's response to it, growing up. Or, if following an illness or accident, ask yourself if you have grieved the loss of who you were before. The more you know yourself, the more integrity you will have at every stage of vocation and ministry, and the more you will be able to withstand the system working out your faults and then you can focus on your fulfilment.

Curiosity over my disability has been borderline rude at times. There were expectations that I wouldn't be able to do certain things or, if I couldn't do things in an able-bodied way, it would lack decorum or meaning somehow, when presiding at the Eucharist, for example. I just do things differently – I lean on the altar if needed and raise the host with one hand. I think Jesus would have reclined at dinner, so he probably used one hand too!

Self-awareness has really helped me, especially after becoming a mum – having my son was a catalyst for change. Before I had him I was saying yes to everything, but he made me realise home life could not be put on the back burner, that life as it had been was not sustainable or fair. However, there were a lot of expectations that I would stay full-time and it was not easy to work out a new pattern for us as a family. I was the first incumbent to go on maternity leave in my diocese and it could have been handled better.

In ministry life, it made me concentrate on only saying yes to things I could do that I was really good at. My son became part of ministry life – I sit to lead or preach and often he would come and sit on my lap while I did so or he'd join me at the altar, which modelled something completely different to my congregations. He became a catalyst for smiles in a church that had previously not been all that smiley. Watching them soften was a joy.

I believe that trying to blend in is not what God called any of us to do. In my experience the individuality of my life has had an impact on people's lives, as I'm sure it will for you too.

If there is anywhere on earth a lover of God who is always kept safe, I know nothing of it, for it was not shown to me. But this was shown: that in falling and rising again we are always kept in that same precious love.

(JULIAN OF NORWICH)

5

Formation or transformation?

BEING INTENTIONAL ABOUT CHANGE

'Gosh, you've changed!' an old friend noted on seeing me for the first time in years. I was 40-something, I'd travelled the world, had three kids, become a Christian and trained to be a vicar. I'm not sure anyone could go through all that *without* changing! Contemplating these changes, as I approached my soon-to-be associate vicar role, I found myself flicking through the pages of my fuchsia pink bullet journal and was drawn to the phrase 'be intentional'. In turquoise felt tip, I had scripted it across the page to remind myself that it is my choice what kind of leader I am. We all change, we are all formed or transformed by what we experience and I made a choice, some time back, that I wanted to be a willing participant in that process.

It wasn't always that way. This is a process that at theological college was always referred to as the dreaded 'formation'. In church terms, formation seems to refer to anything you have to go through during ministerial development that is not much fun. As I flicked through my journal, I was reminded of the first time that I heard the word, at my first ever evening at 'vicar school'. The principal decided that this bunch of ordinands, who had never met before, would perform an icebreaker task, thus provoking a chill of fear to blow through even the hardened extroverts in the room. And fear we should rightly have had, because the task was to imagine an animal to represent the state of the Church of England. Not so bad, you think? Well, he then proceeded to ask us to find anyone else in the room with the same animal by pretending to be that animal [*dies inside at the memory*].

The weekend continued in an ominous vein, staying in an ancient priory where the food was referred to by our tutors as 'curious'; the rooms had just one plug socket – so you could have light, heat, charger *or* hair straighteners and the shower room had enormous holes in the ancient wooden panelling. Not sure what it says about my formation that I chose hair straighteners over heat . . .

Formation to me implies an end goal, a finished product, as though with enough experiences we'll become the perfect ministers. The reality, I think, is more *transformation*, that as we go through life, both as mums and as ministers, we are continually being transformed. Sometimes this happens gradually, sometimes dramatically; at times it can be unnoticed, at others blindingly obvious. Fighting against change or refusing to acknowledge challenges is probably not going to be all that helpful in ministry – every minister is going to face challenge and change in their lives. Perhaps *formation* is all about letting those situations *transform* us into better ministers, parents, friends and colleagues, and more into the likeness of Christ.

Life and death

Like my icebreaker challenge though, sometimes when an opportunity to be formed comes along, it's uncomfortable, hard to engage with or perhaps raises emotions in us we'd rather not deal with. The chances are we are not alone in that. One trainee minister who was going through a really difficult time at college reminded me that the more vulnerable you can be in sharing your own story, the more you find others feeling that way too. Our formational experiences will vary depending on our own life experiences and ministry, but that shared vulnerability can produce a sense of solidarity, compassion or mutual support. One experience that might be shared by many of us is funerals.

Though it sounds clichéd, I find taking funerals is an absolute privilege. Dying is not a simple business: from death certificates to choosing a funeral director; knowing what happens to the body; where to have the funeral, burial or cremation; wills and probate; letting people know . . . You'd think it would be hard enough dealing with the pain of losing someone, but then suddenly there is a barrage of things to do that most of us don't realise need to happen until the time comes. Something I've come to realise is that if we, as ministers, can help make part of that both simple and meaningful, helping loved ones to say that final goodbye in a way they will remember, then we are doing a good job.

Dealing with other people's grief and pain can be emotionally tough on us but something that I have found transformative. I find professionalism helps me come alongside people in the times of their deepest grief, knowing that I am there to help focus the mind on the what, how and when, rather than the emotions. In spite of this, every so often one might come along to test us more than we can bear: a child, a tragic death, someone taking their own life, or perhaps for some of us a personal experience of loved ones dying can make it even harder.

For me, the hardest yet was helping put together the funeral of a young mum, who left three very young children. In the planning of it, spending time with them, meeting their favourite toys and laughing with them as I would my own kids, the professional veneer was torn down. Later, as we stood outside the church waiting as mummy was brought in, one child held in her father's arms, another holding granny's hand, perhaps not fully understanding, but knowing something was not as it should be, I felt something break in my heart. Perhaps it was in the recognition of love that I know she had for those girls, so full of life and laughter; perhaps it was in seeing the pain of loss played out in front of my eyes, but my job was to help them through this. Later though, as people left the church I found the tears welling and jammed my nail into the palm of my hand to give a quick sharp burst of pain to jolt me back into professional mode. When the last person left, I legged it to the vestry as quick as I could as the floodgates opened. I don't know the pain of losing a child or a mother, but I know what it means to love and be loved, and in that moment I just wanted to scoop up my children and never let go. As I arrived home, my oldest daughter came up and gave me the biggest of hugs as I sobbed, 'I love you so much.' She seemed to know instinctively what I needed, hugging me, bringing me tea and then sitting me down to watch *RuPaul's Drag Race*. Yes, I know, as unlikely as it may seem, it was possibly exactly what I needed in that moment, some frivolity and sequins, sitting in the company of my own precious daughter.

For you, the necessary aftercare of something difficult might be a glass of something, a cuppa with a friend or a long walk. Whatever it is, learning to look after ourselves in formation is vital. Perhaps only those who deal with personal situations like these will understand how they can affect us – people like counsellors, medical staff and, of course, funeral directors who in this line of work we deal with regularly. In this case, it was the wonderful Grace who understood as we worked side by side and who emailed me later to say, 'Bottle of wine tonight?' She gets it. Even as professionals and with experience, I don't think we can fail to be transformed by experiences like these. I know I've realised that when people are facing the most difficult situations, often we just need to be present and to listen. A friend going through cancer treatment told me how lonely she felt because people who knew her just didn't know what to say so they avoided her, when really she didn't want to talk about cancer all the time – she just wanted company or fun or a hug. Transformation for me has meant learning sometimes I need to shut up and often just show up.

Rising and falling

Formation is not like going to college, passing modules and coming out the end with a qualification – it's much more likely to be a life-long process with peaks and troughs. Julian of Norwich, anchorite mystic of the fourteenth century quoted at the start of this chapter, reminds us of this. No matter what we face, we are always in that precious love of God. If we can hang on to these words, knowing that whatever we face is done in the company of God, it might make the process of transformation a little bit easier to bear or perhaps even to embrace.

In 2 Corinthians, Paul writes about the confidence we can have in Christ and how he is at work in us by his Spirit. His line in 3.18 (NIV) is almost a rally cry: 'And we all . . . are being transformed into his image with ever-increasing glory, which comes from the Lord, who is the Spirit.'

As we seek God, the Holy Spirit is transforming us more and more into the likeness of Christ, with, one hopes, ever increasing glory. It might be hard to see sometimes, especially as I'm pretty sure Christ never had to preach after an hour's sleep and with breast milk leaking through his cassock, but thankfully it is the same Holy Spirit who worked through him who works in us too. I have found some of the times when I felt I had nothing left to give, to be those when the Holy Spirit works best. Recently, after a week filled with evening events, followed by an all-day Saturday training course (on a three-line whip from the bishop), I then had to take four services on a Sunday, starting work at 7 a.m. and finishing at 8.30 p.m. I went to the final service that day wondering why I wasn't dead on my feet. Truth is, it was only through God. It is so often in our own weakness that God is strongest (2 Corinthians 12.9–10). For me, formation has had so much to do with acknowledging what I lack and recognising what Jesus brings – daily – heck, *hourly*. Following Jesus' leading is the most transformational thing we can do as we learn from him and are led by him.

I love the stories we read of the disciples in the Bible who spent time personally with Jesus and went on a huge journey of transformation with, let's face it, many rises and falls. Simon Peter, for example, started out as a fisherman, obeyed the call to follow Jesus, even had his name changed and expressed his wholehearted devotion to Jesus and this new life of ministry with him. This must have been a hugely formational experience for him and yet he still denied Jesus in his hour of need. Probably didn't seem all that transformed in that moment, right? But Jesus later asks him to feed his sheep (John 21), allowing him to be transformed again through redemption and setting the tone for Peter's life leading this new church.

Like Peter, our formation will be lifelong with transformational experiences along the way, which we need to navigate. For mums and ministers these experiences, these rises or falls, will be vast and varied but bring us the opportunity to grow in who we are, in wisdom and grace, hopefully becoming more Christlike as we go.

Family formation

Newly pregnant, someone shared with me an updated version of the oft-used Nora Ephron quote: 'Having a baby is like throwing a hand grenade into a relationship and waiting for it to explode.' The same might be said of ministry or any major life change. It's really important not to underestimate how much being in ministry might affect our partners and families in their own formation.

That goes for partners and families who are not Christians too, whose journey through all this peculiar formation business is quite possibly even harder. It's hard enough to get our own heads around the frequently bonkers world of the Church when *we* know we are doing it for Jesus, but, for those who are not even sure Jesus exists, it must seem at times like utter madness. They might have to put up with an in-depth interview with a vocational advisor in the early stages – just to make sure they aren't going to be a newspaper headline waiting to happen, I suppose; they put up with moving, probably many times; they deal with bishops, moderators and any number of other oddly titled roles with politeness and aplomb, even though they've heard the gossip and it's distinctly unchurchy.

Having a partner who does not share your faith *can* be a real positive though. Ministry mums have pointed out that it is easier to draw stricter boundaries around work and home life, and put realistic expectations in place with the church, with a partner who doesn't attend. One shared how her non-Christian husband was great at getting her head out of the parish regularly because he didn't share in her experiences within it and another noted that it gave a completely different dimension to the way she ministers.

However, some ministry mums have noted the difficulties of being a minister with a partner who is not a Christian; for example, not being able to pray together, the partner not being able to understand that it's a calling rather than 'a job' or having differing moral views. We hope that our partners' and families' experience of transformation might also be positive but unfortunately it isn't always. I've sadly heard more than one story from church leaders whose partners' faith or relationship with the church has been affected by seeing the other side of ministry. One church leader told me how the pressure of ordained life hastened the end of her marriage, with the strain of not being able to talk about faith with a husband who didn't share her beliefs and the pressures of carrying the load of ministry alone being key factors.

For our children, the intensity of formation is already even greater as they simply grow older, each year bringing dramatic change both mentally and physically. I believe one of our roles as parents is in discipling them in the spiritual journey, as well as the physical and mental one. Over the years, as a family we've used/tried/given up on/thrown away/embraced various ways of actively discipling our kids as they have grown and as their own questions have arisen. From active prayer times when they were little – getting creative, building stuff, throwing stuff and making prayer boxes – to Bible study with 'lift the flap' Noah's Ark and *Veggie Tales*; to *The Street Bible*, *The Message* and, more recently, the *Youth Bible* – we've tried a lot. One of our favourites, thanks to Miranda Threlfall-Holmes' *Teenage*

Prayer Experiment (2015), was building a Minecraft prayer space that had them occupied for days with so much thought and care built into those virtual holy spaces. We will probably all approach the discipling of our children in different ways. One mum pointed out to me that being led by our own children's curiosity and listening to their questions and observations no matter how simplistic they may seem can be an excellent starting point for approaching their spiritual transformation. They often understand far more than we give them credit for.

One Methodist ministry mum shared with me how important it is for her children to experience spirituality and that we need to remember even very young children can have an understanding of symbolism and worship. She recounted how, at a recent baptism service, they had prepared a pile of rocks for people to take symbolically and her two-year-old decided that she was going to kneel and hand a stone to everyone as they came forward. It was, she says, a moving gesture of diaconal service from a child who demonstrated she understood the moment. This ministry mum's oldest child now receives Communion and has been heard to exclaim, 'Great job' Jesus' on receiving the bread! As she points out, kids get ritual and sacrament – they just need the details explaining. My youngest child is very creative and when she was really quite little she began to draw as a way of expressing what she was feeling of God. Though simple, her pictures spoke to me of her spirituality in a way she wasn't able to explain for herself in words. As a mum, my sense of nurturing that gift in her is just as strong as the desire to nurture those I minister to at church.

Of course, as they grow they will make their own decisions both in life choices and in what they believe and our influence upon their formation will decrease (though I don't think it ever goes away entirely). For me, though, the non-negotiable factor in this process is in praying for them – even when they've hurt us or when we might not want to be in the same room as them. Without getting overly spiritual here, I think many of us would say that our kids are the ones who bring us the biggest joy but probably the biggest anxiety too and because of that I think that the devil uses them to get to us. Praying for them and for God's presence in their lives is, at the very least, a defence and, at the most, watering their souls.

Being a minister's kid is not easy – so often, I wonder if the amount of time they spend at church puts them off, or whether the questions from congregation members, the upheaval of moving house or the amount of time work keeps me away from them gives them a negative view. You can imagine my delight therefore on hearing the words from my son, 'Mum, I think I want to be baptised.' Although I'm sure time spent talking about faith, reading the Bible together, praying and going to church had had an impact on him, it was away from us that he really met the Lord. At two separate Christian camps one summer he had powerful encounters with God that gave him his own personal connection with Jesus and he wanted to stand up and say so. At our church we offer full immersion baptism and, standing in the water with him, signing him with the cross, seeing him go under the water and coming out with the biggest smile on his face was just, well, it's hard to find the words. The best way to describe it, I think, is in the metaphor that Jesus uses of giving birth, being born again. Just as I gave birth to him – in pain, in blood, sweat and tears, with hard work and determination and so much love – getting to that point of baptism was a labour of sorts too. It held that same joy of new life being born, that same rush of love, that same letting go of breath: it is done.

Mentally loaded?

In the same way our spiritual formation has an impact on our family, our family's growth, in turn, provides new opportunities for our own. It can, for example, decrease our 'mental load'. I was introduced to this concept, highlighted by French cartoonist Emma in her feminist comic, a while back when I came across it in *The Guardian*. Mental load means the mental (and in many cases emotional) responsibility for not just the *doing* of various tasks but the *planning* of them – and in many households, even egalitarian ones, women are taking on the majority of this load. In my case, my husband readily admits that if I didn't do it, lots of things would drop in the immediate term but that, over time, he would realise what needs to be done. I wonder how often we take things on because it's easier to do so, when actually delegating such 'loads' may lead to a better formation for our families?

Encouraging children from a young age to take responsibility for their own things can help them to develop independence, eventually meaning an independence of their own spiritual lives. This can work for our congregations too. Paul talks a lot about the body of Christ being one body with many parts – let's encourage those parts to step into what *they* can do for God's kingdom (and possibly take off our plate!) and help them grow and be transformed in the process. It can be hard for a congregation, who have got used to the way you minister to them without children, to have to face the changes that come with motherhood, and walking the line between taking people with you, and gently encouraging them to change where needed, is a huge part of ministry.

Rt Revd Dr Steven Croft notes in *The Gift of Leadership* that times of transition can be key times of learning. Further, that listening to key voices in those times, especially those of dissent, is important in whatever 'rebuilding' comes next. As ministry mums, for our families and for our congregations, those times of transition might be physical – as it is in pregnancy; practical – as it is when we move house or church; and spiritual – as we are formed and transformed by our experiences.

Being intentional in noticing and navigating such change can be a powerful way to enhance our transformation. I wonder if you've ever taken time to consider the transformational times in your own life and thought about how they have changed you. Have you contemplated the transitions of family life for yourself and those who depend on you? Have you deliberated on how you, as a new minister, are bringing transformation, possibly unwelcome, to a new congregation? In addition, in so many places mothers in ministry are still relatively new, so perhaps part of *our* formation is in helping new systems to be formed or in enabling others to be formed in new ways as they consider different possibilities in the church. And, in doing so, let's not forget the rebuilding – the moving forward, the intentional changes, taking people with us and being led by God in it all.

Jo's story

Jo Patterson is a minister in the United Reformed Church, working in a stipendiary role as a Church Related Community Worker. She is married with two children aged 13 and 18.

❛In the United Reformed Church there are two different types of licensed ministry. I trained as a Church Related Community Worker, which means I combine the ministry of word and theology alongside community work. Interestingly, in the URC, 75 per cent of CRCWs are women.

Candidating (assessment) and then training really was a period of formation for all of us as we worked out what this new way of life would look like as a family. Following assessment, I spent four years in training, which meant travelling to college in Manchester from Kent once a week for academic teaching alongside others, coupled with training in placements closer to home. My husband moved his job closer to home so he could be at home more.

One of the drawbacks of being in an independent church is that churches have different conversations and levels of support when someone from their congregation is training – but I personally have felt hugely supported. During candidating, I was encouraged to think carefully about what ministry life would mean for us as a family. The church I was based in was fully aware of how important my family is and our needs, as well as mine, were discussed with them and taken into account. As a result, this meant that we were all able to grow in the process and the changes it would bring, together.

Normally, after training, ministers go through a "call process" where synods and moderators (area leaders) look at those finishing training and where they might fit best. Colleges write profiles and candidates can add their own and their families' needs too. In fact, my first year placement went so well that the church applied for a CRCW-accredited project and I have been called to serve here. This is a good fit for all of us as a family.

Formation has been a key part of my journey personally. During training we were encouraged to think about it and specifically pointed to placements that might help us to fill gaps in our experience or to think about areas we might not have considered. I spent time in a New Frontiers church, for example, choosing to face those who did not necessarily agree with my ministry. College tutors were also really helpful at reminding us to look at the bigger picture of "whole life ministry" and listen to the world around us – God doesn't want us to be unhappy, after all. I was also encouraged by strong women and tutors at college who taught us how to stand up for ourselves and combat any negative views. The programme at my college included teaching on pastoral boundaries – for us and others – things like managing stress, looking after ourselves in confrontation and conflict transformation.

As a family, communicating well, and often, has been vital. I've always talked to my children about how they felt about decisions that had to be made, making sure they always know I am there to listen. Parenting them properly has to come before ministry and I will always put in time for that. Although they were a bit older when I started training (9 and 14), I can see how they have been formed by the experience and I think it has helped them to be more confident as well. One of the highlights of being a ministry mum was at my commissioning service where my children were actively involved in it and my daughter ended up writing about the service for the church newsletter. Seeing them blossom makes me realise even on the tough days that I'm doing an OK job!'

It is often when night looks darkest, it is often before the fever breaks that one senses the gathering momentum for change, when one feels that resurrection of hope in the midst of despair and apathy.

(HILLARY CLINTON, 2018)

6

Sustainable sacrifice

NOT OFFERING YOURSELF ON THE ALTAR OF MINISTRY

When the bishop's email popped into my inbox inviting me to the clergy conference to be held later that year, I had mixed feelings (and when I say 'invitation' clearly I mean 'summons'). On the one hand, it meant an opportunity to hear some interesting speakers, network, hang out with some ministry colleagues away from the workplace and have some downtime in the bar. But, on the other, it meant sacrificing three days with my family during the first week of the new school year. One of my colleagues even missed their child's first ever day at school.

When the time came, a military operation was in place in our house to make sure everyone was ready: school runs and pickups were planned round my husband's meetings, playdate favours were called in, uniforms were named (stick-on labels of course) and school bags pre-packed. This was not just my sacrifice but the family's too and they made me know about it. 'But *why* do I need to pack *now*?' was heard several times in the week running up to the conference.

This was not the first sacrifice we'd made in ministry, nor would it be the last. In the time I've worked for the Church there have been a whole range of sacrifices from snow days spent taking a burial (in minus temperatures and wellies under the robes!) rather than sledging with the kids, to attending a silent retreat instead of a family fortieth celebration, and not being able to attend numerous kids' sports matches and concerts due to pastoral situations. Saturday nights are now cocktail-less as I await an 8 a.m. BCP or prayer breakfast and big Sunday roasts fade into a full-on workday – perhaps the most stinging of these was having a four-service Sunday while my husband took the kids to a test match, *ouch*. Sacrifice is part and parcel of what it means to be a ministry mum, but perhaps a question we should always ask is whether the sacrifices are worth it – for us, for the children and for the church.

Enforced sacrifice

Though ministry life is far from ordinary and will undoubtedly involve sacrifice, one thing we need to watch for is having sacrifice forced on us. There can be a tendency within the Church to sanctify sacrifice in an unhealthy way with the idea that those who give up the most, or have the hardest time, are the ones closest to God. Sometimes it can be used as a term to accuse ministers of not doing what they should and as women I think we can be particularly susceptible to this. If we find ourselves in old school structures and patriarchal systems, we may feel that we need to do what we're told without challenging the reason why.

Early on in my ministry life, while exploring my vocation, I was told that I would need to leave my church and go to a more traditional one. This would have meant moving my family from a church where we were all being fed spiritually, as well as leaving my job in that church, simply because one man in authority thought it necessary. When I questioned this, I was firmly reminded that sacrifice would be required of me throughout my ministry and that I should consider that a bit more. It was, I felt, a very unfair accusation and so I took some time to pray and think about how I could respond, seeking advice from a mentor. At my next meeting, I was then able to calmly explain why I was not willing to move church and the impact it would have on my family. It was a tricky situation, as I wasn't sure how much impact my reticence to comply would have on my future ministry, but I also knew it was not right for me or my family.

Though we still disagreed, in the end it did not become a sticking point and we stayed.

It seems almost funny to me, as a mum, that I would be accused of refusing to make a sacrifice, because I think for anyone who is a parent, the concept of giving things up for the greater good is hardly a new one. Sleep, for example, in the early months of babyhood (or years, so sorry if that's you), long afternoons at mind-numbing soft-play with balls being thrown at our heads or being taxi-driver to teenagers when they need lifts at 2 a.m. are all sacrifices. Then there are those of us who have sacrificed their role as 'child' in order to look after their own aging parents, often juggled alongside being a parent themselves and a minister. We do these things willingly (well, 2 a.m. call-outs perhaps not *quite* so willingly), because we love our children just as we love Jesus and so are prepared to do the things he asks of us, even when they are firmly not on our personal 'to-do list'. But sacrifice *enforced* upon us just leads to resentment and exhaustion, so we need to find ways to discern carefully, when sacrifice is asked of us, whether the question comes from the church, leadership or actually from God.

Sustainable sacrifice

A concept I find helpful here is 'sustainable sacrifice', as coined by Christopher Ash in his book about avoiding burnout. Sustainable sacrifice reminds us to recognise our *human* needs alongside our *divine* calling. This is so important to hold on to, particularly for us mums, because modern society teaches us that we can be super women. Glossy magazines tell us 'you can have it all!' while showcasing the perfect mum, running her own business selling handwoven yak hair cushions, interviewed while she nonchalantly sips upon a latte on her perfectly positioned sofa – which I notice features no baked bean stains or the merest hint of sacrifice. It's no wonder that working mums find the right life balance unattainable when these are the role models which are highlighted to us. As Ash reminds us, 'God is under no illusions about who he is getting on his team'. Of course not – this is God we are talking about and, thank goodness, God *does* know us inside out. God knew my internal struggle when my phone flashed to life, my heart sinking as I recognised the number and realised I had a choice: spend half an hour having the life sucked from me or ignore the call and spend the same amount of time stewing in shame. I'd like to say this was the first time this had happened, but it's not. I'd like to say that, with Jesus in my heart, I was overwhelmed with compassion and answered right away, but I didn't, letting it ring off before calling them back later. As expected, it was not the easiest of conversations, but the person on the other end was so appreciative of my time and my inadequate words of comfort, that the effort was so worthwhile.

I think that, if we're all honest with ourselves, we know when God is asking something difficult of us, as I did with my phone call, and, as much as we might occasionally want to stick our fingers in our ears and not listen, we know God is going to keep asking. But, in the wisdom of my curacy advisor, 'Offering our lives to God's service does not mean setting aside everything else in life and carrying everything yourself'. Much as I might try to make it so, ministry is not like a to-do list where there is an end in sight at the close of each day. It's usually never-ending, so the sacrifices we make need to be sustainable in the long run. If we want to avoid the danger of sacrificing ourselves on the altar of ministry, giving in to the accusations or requests, or the never-ending list of tasks, then reminding ourselves that God knows us completely, sees our struggles and loves us all the same, might be helpful.

Equally, having someone who can help you to keep your sacrifices in sensible measure can be really helpful – a critical friend, mentor, partner – someone who you know will give you a kick up the rear when needed, but also someone who can bring a gentle and loving reminder of all that is important in our lives. I'm a big fan of mentoring and meet up with mine once a term. He's an excellent cheerleader, as well as someone who can challenge me when I'm holding my own personal pity party about the sacrifices I am currently making.

Beautiful sacrifice

Truly and wisely offering our lives to God's service will mean some tough choices at times and the need to step into things we feel unprepared for. But it isn't always in the grand gestures of sacrifice and self-giving where God is at work; sometimes it's in the *smallest* of observations where I find God reminds me of the power of sacrifice.

Exhausted, having been up half the night with a poorly child, and not feeling at all like serving God, I found myself weeping at the altar rail during one early morning service. 'The body of Christ, broken . . . for . . .' My voice cracked as I looked down into a pair of huge, roughened and calloused working hands. I was reminded of *the* carpenter's hands and the wounds that united us there in that place, in that moment. As I placed the bread into his outstretched palms, it was as if Jesus himself were kneeling before me and my sleepless sacrifice suddenly seemed insignificant. Moving further along the line I whispered for fear of giving way to emotion, 'The body of Christ, broken for you' to a cancer patient; 'The body of Christ, broken for you' to a couple grieving the loss of a child; 'The body of Christ, broken for you' to one whose physical health meant gnarled and bent hands; to another who couldn't manage the steps up to the rail but whose gentle, grateful smile touched my heart: 'The body of Christ, broken for you.' In those moments the sacrifices I make, great and small, are worth everything that I have to offer.

Not sacrificing your family

Finding fulfilment in our calling in those beautiful moments can sustain us, but our sacrifices are not just about us. They affect our partners and families, who may in turn need to make their own sacrifices. When clergy partners were surveyed as part of the 'Experiences of Ministry' project, it was noted that, though largely positive, they admitted to making regular sacrifices for their partner's role and more than half of them agreed that they did not know where their partner's ministry ended and family life began. Even if we feel at the top of our game, if our families are suffering, we might need to step back and take a broader look.

Some of the best advice I've received is to try at all costs to protect time each week with your family, with several ministry mums recommending actually scheduling it in to your diary. Not only does this help you keep the space, but also allows you to honestly say, 'Oh, I have something in the diary then.' Some even suggested acronyms – helpful if you have a shared work diary – like WFOS meeting – *With Family On Sofa* or TWK – *Time With Kids*. Others recommend taking space when you find it, something we try to do wherever possible, so an unexpected free Sunday afternoon becomes an opportunity to do something fun rather than filling it with work. Of course, avoid the pressure to *have* to have a wonderful time!

I cringe when I remember an afternoon like this, last summer. 'Let's go out and do something nice,' I suggested, walking in from the last service of the day. I had rather wistful visions of beachside walks, laughing together as we indulged in overpriced seaside ice cream, but the response from my offspring was rather more luddite, a resounding 'no', followed by an 'only if we can . . .' as they recognised a possibility for bargaining. I should have sensed in that moment that things might not quite fit my perfect family vision, but undeterred I dragged everyone off the sofa. Trawling through the Brighton summer traffic, we couldn't even agree on where to go so ended up splitting in two, with one party to minigolf and one to the pier. Twenty pounds in small change later and now equipped with a garishly fluorescent stuffed fish, I fought on like some kind of parent martyr, fighting back the internal tirade of angst as I cheerily suggested,

'Come on, let's go to JoJo's for ice cream.' After a mere 45 minutes deciding that, out of 457 flavours, vanilla was the only one desired – I'm pretty sure only to spite me – we fell back into the car, slightly traumatised. One forced full-on roast dinner later (why I didn't stop at the awful pier-trip was beyond me!), I noticed my daughter scratching her head and the fateful discovery was made of that wonderful family friend, the nit; except, of course, it wasn't just one, but a blinking army of the little blighters.

By the time everyone was deloused and in bed we were exhausted, which leads me on to . . . [*mouths*] sex. Let's face it, once the metaphorical stork has arrived, the bedroom is never going to be the same again. The glow of being in love and passionate, lingering embraces turns into a quick grope when the little ones are asleep, desperately hoping that the baby doesn't wake up, the toddler doesn't wander in at an inopportune moment or the teenager doesn't barge in oblivious, needing to borrow a charger. And that's assuming you even have the energy anyway. Then there's the distractions of life. Not long ago, we were walking home hand in hand after a meal out, with the slight afterglow of a bottle of rosé. My mind was wandering to what might happen when we got home when suddenly my husband blurted out: 'Oh shit! I didn't finish the Asda order . . . Never mind I'll finish it in bed.' I laughed out loud, to which he responded, '#AsdaForeplay.' He wasn't joking either. Twenty minutes after getting into bed, he was still tapping away on the iPad and turned to me to ask if I needed any feminine care products. He's a keeper. In all seriousness, though, don't let your sex life be one of the sacrifices! Find those opportunities where and when you can, even if that means 'working from home' from time to time when no one else is around . . .

Sacrificial trigger points

The sacrifices we make in ministry life will vary, but I know that moving house is one of those biggies for many people. Moving home and starting a new job are commonly referred to as being among the top ten most stressful life situations to go through and yet, for many of us in ministry, we do both at the same time, often coupled with a change of childcare and/or school for our kids too.

Without a doubt, there is a financial sacrifice to moving home, which can be especially so in a non-stipendiary role. It's worth asking what the financial expectations are in advance, from removal fees – which can be covered by the church in some denominations – to who pays for what in the house itself. We received a grant from our diocese when we moved to our current home but ended up having to spend much of it on carpets as the existing ones were bug-infested! If you are lucky enough to get a grant like this at any stage I'd suggest being really wise with it and investing in things you might not be able to afford on a minister's pay. For me, this meant decent study furniture that I knew would last and a good printer – the bane of many a minister's life. A printer that works well is like a little angel in your office.

Another trigger point that will affect many of us and our families is the change of childcare and schools. Sacrificing a wonderful childminder or the proximity to grandparents and starting the search all over again for a job move, is not to be underestimated in the stress stakes! For a start, don't assume that moving to a new parish with a church school means an automatic place for your child; it usually doesn't even for Church of England ministers. This issue has been raised at General Synod in recent years and it was agreed to lobby for the same rights as others who are deployable or in tied accommodation, so watch this space. That said, I have heard a few examples where there has been some flexibility depending on the LEA or governing body, so it's always worth pushing a bit. Finding special schools adds in further complications and stress, and a new role can mean the sacrifice for the whole family of a good school nearby for one much further away or one that is less suitable.

There are some independent schools that offer assisted places for ministers' children, which might be something to think about if you feel that is right for you, though do be aware of extra costs; even with a full bursary there are things that will be more pricey – like more expensive uniform, school buses, which are not subsidised, and school trips.

Sacrifices like these can be incredibly draining for the whole family, with so many new things to encounter and work through, often in isolation as we move away from those we know and love. We've found that perhaps the biggest trigger point for all of us has been the sacrifice of an immediate support system and friendships with those with whom we were doing 'life together'. It's been really tough for us in times of huge transition like this where we have needed to focus on our kids a bit more to help them through the sacrifices *they* are making while battling through it ourselves with little support.

As we prepared to move on from one church, coming down the hall one Sunday, I saw in front of me the banner advertising our children's ministry featuring a photo of my children happily playing with their friends. It was as if that picture was mocking my inner turmoil, a stark reminder of all that we were sacrificing as a family, all that had been built up between us and our friends and in that moment it was just too much for me to bear. Breaking down, I couldn't even lead the service that morning and had to hand over to a colleague as I sobbed in the back room. I felt guilty and ridiculous; why couldn't I pull myself together? I felt exposed. I felt bereft. I felt the rawness of my pain hit me like a sledgehammer. But this is one of the hardest sacrifices of ministry that in forming bonds, in loving others and allowing ourselves to be loved, we make ourselves vulnerable and exposed.

For some of us, and our families, we go through this sacrifice time and again and it can be hard to keep opening up, keep seeking to form new bonds when we know at some point they will be changed or broken. But I do think it is vital for our own well-being, and that of our families, to have people who can help sustain and support us, as well as laugh and have fun with us. In any new role, one of my first prayers is that God will bring people alongside us in that place. People who we can trust, who we can have fun with, who don't just want to be friends with the minister or the pastor's kids, those who are not going to repeat things we've said in confidence or gossip about us behind our backs.

Such changes can, of course, have a massive impact on our children. I've heard many stories about teenagers particularly resenting their parents, the church and the ministry role because they have had to move away from what they know. Rob Parsons notes in his book *Teenagers! What every parent has to know* (an excellent read) that, although teens can present as cocky and self-assured, inwardly they are desperately trying to make sense of their journey into independence. Add into that a house move, school move or both and there is huge potential for fireworks. The best advice I was given on this is that it's vital to continue to invest in our relationships with our teens as they grow and to always remember to be the adult. I regularly remind myself that just because they are becoming more independent and less focused on us, it doesn't mean they don't want us around. One ministry mum colleague was questioned about why she needed to do the school run when her children were old enough to get home from school by themselves, but it was a key expectation both she and her kids had, that she would be able to pick them up. I find some of the best conversations I have with my children are on the school run. It's as if, in that space, when there is not the distraction of the X Box, their brains start to unload and unwind, and all manner of things come out. Ongoing communication with our children when navigating these 'family sacrifices' is vital.

It was about two years into my current post, when I suddenly realised we had friends who supported us as a family. A night of dinner and singing Britney Spears and the Levellers over coffee-flavoured tequila (for info, this is definitely not recommended) cemented a new friendship, with our children having similar moments of realisation with new friends too (and a little less tequila, I hope!) Some of those friendships will be formed over years and will last through several moves; others are for a season, but both are crucial to sustaining us in all we do.

Trusting in the ultimate sacrifice

All these things are essentially about putting our trust in where God leads; they may be a sacrifice, but they are done for the one who made the *ultimate* sacrifice. We know that Jesus made that ultimate sacrifice for us in love and trusting in the truth of that love amid all that we face is something we regularly preach to others, but perhaps need to be reminded of ourselves occasionally. Jesus called us to love church but also to love our families and ourselves. When he said 'love your neighbour . . .' he also said '. . . as yourself'. So, when King Solomon says in Proverbs 3.5–6 that we should trust the Lord with all our hearts, he isn't saying just walk blindly off into the sunset and tell everyone it's all for him and it will all be fine; he's talking about listening to God and being guided by God. *The Message* puts those verses like this:

> Trust GOD from the bottom of your heart;
> don't try to figure out everything on your own.
> Listen for GOD's voice in everything you do,
>   everywhere you go;
> he's the one who will keep you on track.
> Don't assume that you know it all.
> Run to GOD! Run from evil!

If a potential sacrifice is on the table, then let's take it to God and ask, 'Is this really what is being asked of us?' Listening to God's voice might help with opportunities that come our way too. Chances to preach in other places, to be involved in wider events or ministries, or roles with more responsibility can all be attractive, but might not be what God is leading us to. I've found, at times, that my own enthusiasm can get in the way of God's promptings, leading to a tired and overworked Jules making unnecessary sacrifices in order to keep it all going.

I find the words from Hillary Clinton quoted at the start of this chapter helpful – that it is often in the darkness when hope might shine. I expect we can all cite hardships we have been through that have drawn us closer to Christ, and others that have sent us reeling away from him. But Clinton's words remind me that he is with us even in the darkest times. Isn't that what Psalm 23 tells us anyway? In those times, in the darkest depths of our soul, even a glimmer of hope can bring amazing clarity.

Clinton suggests that it's in that moment before change, before resurrection dawns, that things seem darkest; we know this to be true for the disciples after Jesus died, as they wondered if death had won. But then that glorious ray of hope dawned as the women saw the empty tomb and they rushed off to share this glimmer of hope after desolate pain.

For some of us, the call to sacrifice will be greater or harder to bear and there will be times when we need to run to God in the pain of sacrifice, both from the smaller sacrifices to those that are all-consuming. Ruth's story, at the end of this chapter, highlights the sacrifice of spending months away from her children as an RAF chaplain; others have shared how the sacrifice of ministry affected their marriage and there are those who are dealing with loss, pain and grief, having to sacrifice a personal place for grief while working in a public-facing role. Perhaps for some of you reading this, the personal sacrifice right now seems hard to bear. Whatever your situation, I'm convinced that the only way we can get through this crazy life we are called to is with Jesus at our side, our guide and our strength, trusting in a God who made the ultimate sacrifice for each of us. That sacrifice was given in overwhelming love and meant facing overwhelming darkness, but we know the end of the story too – that love wins. So whatever sacrifices you face, never forget to seek God in the darkness – sometimes it's when hope shines brightest.

Ruth's story

Revd (Wing Commander) Ruth Hake MBE is an ordained Church of England minister who has served for the last 15 years as an RAF chaplain. She is married to Bryan, an RAF officer and they have two children, aged seven and ten.

❝I have always had elements of sacrifice in my role, even before having children – as an RAF chaplain I am posted abroad on a regular basis, which can be tough. Having children obviously made that more of a sacrifice but then I was ordained seven years before I became a mum, so I try and think about how parenting fits with my existing ministry life rather than the other way around.

In many ways this is a sacrifice for the kids too as we move house a lot and I can also be away from them for months at a time. Perhaps the hardest time was just after having my first son and I was posted to the Falklands where there was no childcare, no nappies and no baby milk! In the end, my mum travelled 8,000 miles to come and look after my son.

Childcare is always tricky and, as we move every eighteen months to two years, there is a constant need to find the 'next' solution. There is rarely childcare available on a Sunday and my husband doesn't usually attend church so I often end up ministering with them in tow. I am well used to presiding while having one or other of them on my hip, and once had someone come to me after a Remembrance Service after I had glared my "Paddington Hard Stare" at my son during the silence so effectively that this individual came to me to explain that children didn't always understand that they needed to be quiet during a silence. I then had to explain that I didn't care what every other child in the place did – but the one diving into the raked-up leaves by the war memorial was actually mine! The added complication now they are a bit older is schooling and my kids have moved school a lot, sometimes with very little notice; that's the nature of military life.

However, despite the sacrifices, there are lots of positives too. My work is hugely fulfilling with daily pastoral contact with many people of all faiths and none. On a practical level my working hours are normally daytime, roughly 7.30 a.m. – 5 p.m.; outside of that there is very little work, aside from an 'on-call' responsibility. By and large, I get home every day in time for tea and bedtime, and my evenings are my own. Weekends are similar: I nearly always get Saturday completely free and Sunday is, at most, one service (about half the time this service is taken by a colleague so I am free to simply attend or be elsewhere).

In addition, our home is our home and not my workplace. People don't pop in and I have no meetings there – my office is elsewhere. Having grown up in a vicarage, I can't tell you how great I think this is! I relax at home and switch off from work in a way that I don't think I ever saw my dad do.

Things that keep me going are: having a sense of humour, holding lightly to other people's opinions about how one parents or ministers and gin. ❯

Sabbath is a prescription for the relief of heaviness that threatens to overtake you.

(SHELLY MILLER, 2016)

7

Prayer and Prosecco

GETTING REST AND RECREATION

'Thank you, Jesus,' I murmured as I sipped on a cold, crisp glass of Prosecco, the sun going down, waves lapping in the distance and not a shouted 'MUM' to be heard. After years of battling retreat centres, I had realised that I just don't like them and instead booked myself an Airbnb on the coast for my annual retreat. For the first time, I had also packed a bottle of wine along with my Bible and hadn't felt a jot of guilt. I went running, read God's word, prayed and switched off. In those few days on the coast I felt more rested than I had in years, more in touch with my identity and I heard from God in a powerful way.

Ever since that retreat, I've realised that for me there are two key elements to rest, which enable me to thrive. Perhaps they will strike a chord with you too. First, I need time to focus on God without distractions and, second, I need time to do what I love – recreation time, perhaps otherwise known as: prayer and Prosecco. I believe we all need both – time where we can actively rest in God's presence, taking time to seek God in prayer, but also downtime (of course, God is still with us in all things) when we can switch off and do something we love (not necessarily fuelled by Prosecco!) I find these times of rest need to punctuate my day, week and life, not just when I head off for retreat, thoroughly exhausted. I know, I know! I can hear you now – 'easier said than done!' For many ministers, times of rest end up at the bottom of the pile and we even forgo our 'retreat time' entitlement; there is just too much to be done. We give out, give out, give out and we wear ourselves down. When I am too tired,

I turn into some kind of mum-zilla and get very crotchety; suddenly the cushions being out of place is incredibly irritating and the shoe that has been in the doorway for a week may end up going for a short flying lesson. The family have learned not to engage with me at these times, avoiding eye contact at all cost. Even the cat steers clear. But this is not the me I want to be. This is not the me standing in my God-given identity I have come to know and love. This is not the life I want to model to my family.

How about you? Do you ever get to those points of being run down? What are your signs of not having rested enough? I wonder when the last time you took some time to sit down was: to rest; to recharge; to reflect. When did you last take time out to think and pray about how you are doing, how you are feeling? That might be on retreat and having some time away, or it might be in taking a morning to pray or, quite likely with young children, it might just be taking a short moment: a selah pause perhaps.

Selah pause

A few years back, God introduced me to the word 'selah' and it's now one of my favourite words in the Bible! Even the sound of it makes me want to sigh deeply as I breathe it out. We don't truly know the meaning of the word, but the description I favour most is one that suggests a pause or rest, a break in proceedings to reflect. Possibly a musical term or an indication to musicians, it features through-out the Psalms and one can imagine perhaps a stop to take a breath before continuing. It's a word that has really spoken to me; it says something of taking time to reflect on where God is, in our rest and in our lives. It's also a word that I have found really helpful as I have grappled with rest and recreation in ministry, finding it hard to stick to longer times of rest. Remembering each day to take just a moment is something I *can* do, asking myself: where is God at work and what is God saying to me right now?

At the risk of sounding like an internet-spawned inspirational self-help graphic, why not take a short selah pause right now? Find a comfy chair, grab a cuppa (or coffee, Prosecco, chocolate – your choice) and take a moment. Stop reading and just check in with God. Sip your coffee and ask yourself about your own well-being.

Sabbath reality?

One step further than selah is Sabbath. Sabbath rest is really overlooked in the contemporary world. The biblical concept of taking a day a week to do nothing except worship, rest and be with those we love is almost impossible to attain now and, for ministers, even more so. Sunday in our house means running between services, hopefully squeezing in a shared family lunch at some point, and Saturdays are not much better, as they can be filled with anything from house shopping to kids' sports matches, birthday parties and friends' play-dates, because it's the only day those things can happen. For me, it's also still a workday, which regularly means finishing the sermon for Sunday. Not exactly what I'd call restful.

My friend Shelly Miller has an amazing attitude to Sabbath. A few years back she realised that she wasn't really resting or taking time out. Her mind never switched off from daily life, but she had stopped thinking about the motivation behind it all. She decided a change was needed and started 'Sabbath Society'. In her exploration of Sabbath, she encourages others to seek to find *their* Sabbath rest in whatever form it takes for them personally, but particularly in thinking about how we use Sabbath to relate to God. I love her description of Sabbath as a 'prescription for the relief of heaviness that threatens to overtake you . . .' As a busy mum, writer and married to H, a vicar, she knows that threat of heaviness all too well. In their times of Sabbath they go as far as eating off paper plates sometimes in order not to wash up, computers are turned off to limit distraction and laundry is left undone. Now, if we did that in our house, we'd never have clean clothes and my eco-side would resent the paper plates, but it works for them and that is vital. How about asking yourself what Sabbath rest might look like for you and your family? Where is the time to be with God, to worship and pray? Where is the time to be together, to rest and have fun with one other?

The day off

All this leads into the 'day off', aka 'the rest day' as it is known in some denominations. Some of us work six days a week; some of us juggle self-supporting ministry with secular work; and many of us are Jesus Jenga Juggling it all with family too. I find the term 'rest day' amusing – my days off are usually filled with all the things I can't do the rest of the week – things we term in this home *household admin.* It sounds rather grand and important but actually means all the boring stuff like checking the school diary events, replying to personal emails, sorting out the car insurance or replacing the light bulb in the downstairs loo that has been dodgy for six months. Plus trying to do any of this with small children in tow is probably anything *but* restful. I found a new low, a few years back, when I caught myself fantasising about what it would be like to go to the supermarket *without* a small child in tow. Really, is that the best I can dream of now?

I'm not sure there is a 'best' time for rest or for your day off. It might seem like the obvious choice is Saturday, especially if you have a partner who works weekdays or the kids are school age – then it can mean a day to be together. But this doesn't work if you can't afford childcare all week and your partner being at home means one less day to pay for care; nor if you are a last-minute finisher and need that time to finish Sunday's sermon; nor during wedding season; at any time near Christmas; or if Saturday would be a day spent running the children to various events and activities.

Currently I have Monday as my day off, which seems to be common among ministers with older children. It works well for us because

Saturdays are fairly full with kids' activities anyway, so my husband runs them around and I try to work a light day and we all spend the late afternoon/evening together. The church I currently work at has up to six services on a Sunday of which I'm usually at three or four, meaning I'm nearly always busy until the evening service has finished, so by Monday I'm pretty whacked. When the children were younger, I spent my time off playing with wooden trains, taking long afternoons at the park and having fun with friends until the kids were worn out, and leaving the household jobs undone. Now, days off during the school holidays mean an opportunity to get the kids off any tech devices and go out and do something together – with mixed success!

Energised or drained?

I was pondering the theme of rest a while back with my spiritual director, who suggested that I should learn what things energise me and what drain me, and in those I would find the balance between work, rest and play (to quote a once well-known chocolate ad).

Funerals are a key one for me – even with a relatively straight-forward one, an older person who has had a good life, for example, I find the sense of pressure to do it well quite tiring. I have learned that going straight to a school run from a funeral is not a good move and my kids bear the brunt of my needing to wind down.

The school gate is an interesting one too – is it ministry or is it being a mum? Often both and, rather like Marmite, you either love or hate it. I know some love this interaction and find it a missional opportunity, while others want to get in and out in record timing, without making eye contact, feeling drained by the daily experience.

Being aware of what energises us can help to get a good balance too; for me, seeing friends, writing, reading and running are my go-to restful activities and I know I'll feel better having time doing any of them. One thing I really enjoy is cooking, but most of the time supper means one of us frantically cobbling something together that involves pasta in 20 minutes. On my day off, however, I can spend some time trying out a new recipe or baking something. Yes, I know this might sound rather non-twenty-first-century-woman and I almost don't want to include it, but I genuinely enjoy it when I have the time, and that's the key.

Some other things that *drain* me are: trying to keep up with the fitness tracker, again; watching trash TV when I should be in bed; too much red wine; not enough red wine; Google calendar mishaps; kids remembering things they want to talk about at 10 p.m.; last-minute sermonising; 6.30 a.m. starts for school runs and three pastoral meetings on the trot . . .

Some other things that *energise* me are: a long walk on the South Downs; lazing in beach sun; dinner with the family; having a good old rant to my husband about something unjust; bedtime stories and hugs; writing *what I call* witty 'out of office' emails.

What about you? What are the things that drain *you?* There will always be things that consume us and sometimes we just have to do them – like getting up with the baby or doing a hospital visit. So we might ask ourselves, are there ways in which we can put a structure in place to help us deal with how they drain us? What can you put in place to help you either avoid them, if at all possible, or to help you find them less draining? What are the things that energise you? What things give you joy or bring light to your day? I recommend putting some of these into your diary to remind you to actually do them.

Finding that quiet time

Prayer and time with God have always been a foundation of life for me, not just because I'm a minister, but because I am a lover of Jesus and seeking to be more like him. But, as any busy mum will know, those times can so easily get squeezed because there are so many demands on our time. The 'quiet times' we used to have, or the hours spent reading theological books because we wanted to, are gradually, or heck, suddenly, torn away from us when children become part of our lives and it can be so hard to find a way to bring them back. I even find that, now, during school holidays. I have a term-time routine which works so well and I get to have some quiet time to read and pray the moment the children leave the house, so it takes me a good week to stop resenting that I don't have that time once school breaks up.

With babies, there was even less time for it. Mum-lifestyle books often encourage us to make sure we have 'me time', as if we could carve out a quick trip to the spa whenever we fancy! The reality is, often, that the baby years mean we rarely have the time to even sit down with a cuppa, let alone drink it before it goes cold. So often, especially when my children were younger, I'd sit down to pray or get into bed intending to read my Bible before going to sleep and would just drop off mid-verse! It might be that you can find ways of taking time to be in God's presence during 'work time'. I try and book in a half day once a month for prayer and reflection – a time when no one else is there to ask about rotas, or sermons or why haven't we got any Coco Pops (ever noticed how they get everywhere like little brown beetles? How do they do it?!) I find those times are precious, even when grasped on to in between school runs and meetings. It might also be that you need to discover new ways of nurturing your faith at different stages of mum life. For me, being outdoors always makes me feel close to God and I have found that walking and running – with a buggy when younger and now running with my teen – can become times to pray and focus on God. In those times of giving myself space, I see God more openly, I can see myself more clearly and the way ahead is more visible.

Getting away from it all

In Mark 6, we read how Jesus sends out the apostles, apparently for the first time, to share the good news of who Jesus is. Later in the same chapter they regather:

The apostles gathered around Jesus and reported to him all they had done and taught. Then, because so many people were coming and going that they did not even have a chance to eat, he said to them, "Come with me by yourselves to a quiet place and get some rest." So they went away by themselves in a boat to a solitary place.'
(Mark 6.30–32 NIV)

They don't have much time before people find them, but the lesson is important. Jesus teaches them that having been out doing the business, and reflecting with him, they then need to rest. We see this time and again, with Jesus withdrawing to spend time in prayer, time away from people, to recharge and be refilled with the Holy Spirit, prepared for the next task. If Jesus – who is actually God – *still* took time out to rest and to pray then I wonder who we think we are if we think we can do ministry or parenthood without following this model.

Now yes, I know, I know – it's very unlikely Jesus had to juggle changing nappies in between his sermon on the mount and healing a leper; nor did he worry about getting the chicken out to defrost before going to take an early morning prayer meeting. And yet, this passage tells us that they were so busy they didn't even have time to eat and that people were following them everywhere; I mean that doesn't actually sound that different from being a mum, does it?!

I love the reminder of Romans 12.11 (MSG): 'Don't burn out; keep yourselves fuelled and aflame.' If we are too exhausted we are going to burn out and end up a pile of cooled ash, but more than that we have a responsibility to ourselves, our families and our churches to keep ourselves fuelled so that we can continue to give out all that we need to.

Retreat time

Now that we've looked at the important command of rest, let me ask you, when was the last time you took a retreat? In the Methodist

Church, ministers are entitled to quarter days – three days off together each quarter on top of annual leave, which sounds like a jolly good idea that I am going to recommend to my boss at my next line management meeting. In the CofE we are entitled to take six days each year paid retreat time and it's similar for Baptist ministers, yet so few ministers I know actually take that full allocation.

The reality of being a ministry mum means retreat time away can be problematic, especially so if you have a secular job too, are single or have a partner who works – getting away for a few days is never going to be easy! It can be helpful to challenge our own perceptions of what retreat time should look like. If we've been used to taking time out by ourselves, without having to worry about childcare, then finding an alternative might be a challenge. Try and think outside the box. If you have a baby, is there an option of taking him or her with you? Yes, it might not be as restful as you are used to, but sometimes just being away from work and from home can be enough to help switch your mind off work. One example I heard of was a minister who went to stay with parents who looked after the baby during the day while she was able to pray and reflect, as well as having meals prepared for her. If you have older children, could an event like Spring Harvest or New Wine give an opportunity for you to be filled up, while the kids can go to their own groups?

If getting away *is* your thing, think carefully about where to go. I do know some ministry mums who even manage to go abroad for a few days – nice if you can afford it! Retreat centres, though not *my* fave, can be great and usually have prayer ministers available who can pray with you or guide you in your retreat time. Then there are silent retreats, which I've not done for more than 48 hours, and, to be honest, that was a stretch for someone who likes to talk, but might suit some of us better (probably not ideal with a baby in tow . . .).

If a week is too much in one go, how about spreading it out in two-day chunks across the year? Or, if getting away is impossible, then perhaps just take a few days out of doing the usual ministry stuff to focus on prayer and worship. If you've got childcare anyway for work purposes, you could keep it and spend that time seeking God. One idea I heard about from a few church leaders, is taking a Sabbath week a few times a year – not swiping the diary clear of everything, as enticing as that may sound, but keeping it light and only doing the essentials, allowing space for rest and prayer too. Now, of course, the possibility of this depends on your context and your life situation, but it strikes me as a darned good idea if you can manage it from time to time. As with everything else in this book, the key is to find what works for you rather than trying to conform to an ideal.

Support closer to home

Sometimes it can be helpful to have other people to guide you in your rest or prayer time. That might be on retreat or it might be something closer to home, such as meeting with a spiritual director (apologies if this sounds a bit grand: *'Oh darling, I'm just swanning off for a spot of spiritual direction this afternoon . . .'*). The reality of spiritual direction, for me, is sitting with a rather wonderful wise, old(er) woman, chatting over a cup of Assam (she even introduced me to my favourite tea – that's how good she is) and, just when I get comfortable in the self-indulgent, moany drivel I'm spouting, she metaphorically takes a finger, jabs me in the ribs and points out the rubbish in a single word that I had mentioned 20 minutes previously. Honestly, I don't know how she does it (aside from the Holy Spirit, of course). What's more, and this is the reason for it all, she points me to God – always. She doesn't give me her opinion (except about tea); instead she gently takes hold of my shoulders and turns me a few degrees until I am once again facing Jesus. It's so easy to get swayed by the system; to lose track of what we are called to; to let work take over family time (and let's face it, it's usually that way round); and so easy to lose spiritual focus too. Having someone who can guide you back to the right path or who can suggest resources, ways of praying, or spiritual practices that might help you, is so important.

I know opening up about your inner thoughts might sound like a nightmare to some of us, but good spiritual direction can be an oasis in what is often a crazy busy life. That's not to say it's always going to be easy, probably the opposite in fact, but, as we think about rest and Sabbath, it could be an opportunity for time to step back and reflect, with someone alongside us. For it to work well, you need to find the right person. Some denominations have lists of people they recommend, so you can meet a few and see what works for you. SDs come in different shapes and sizes, so find someone who you can feel comfortable with and are able to be totally open and honest with, though, frankly, I think my SD probably wishes I was slightly *less* open sometimes.

If a spiritual director is just a step too far from you, then ask yourself: who helps you process things when you need to – family, colleagues or friends? Where we each find support will differ and perhaps for different situations we might go to different people. We should also ask ourselves who we rest with. In our Mark passage earlier, we saw the disciples regathering with Jesus and with one other, reflecting and reporting together. Though it might look different, we all need that same support and network around us too, even those of us who are introverts! I have one particular friend, a Christian and a mum, who is probably the only person (aside from my husband) who I know I can share anything with, and I mean *anything*. I know she is totally trustworthy, keeps me accountable and will take anything in her stride, launching into prayer for me. We try and meet once a month and those times of prayer are so precious and at times have kept me going.

We might need official support too. Who do we go to when we need help or advice in a work context? When a colleague is being an ass or a bully? (Yes, ministers can be assholes too I've discovered; yes,

Jesus loves them, of course, but still assholes.) Where do we find that help officially?

Drawing our selah to a close

All of this might sound like a dream, but we do need to remind ourselves to take these moments. Anyone heard the old airline oxygen mask analogy? You need to put on your own oxygen mask before you help anyone else. We will be no good to anyone, family or congregation, if we are worn down and exhausted ourselves. I've seen so many ministers model a way of life that is non-stop, working 60+ hours a week, always being available and never truly resting – for most of us this is unsustainable long term.

When God really spoke to me about the word 'selah', it was during a season of enforced rest and ill health. In that, God reminded me – with what seemed like a loud hailer – that we are made to rest, we are made to spend time with God and we need to pause and stop sometimes, whatever that looks like for each of us. I should admit, though, that I know myself well enough to realise that I need a daily reminder, so I had the word selah tattooed on my wrist to prompt me, whenever I see it, to check myself and check in with God. Bit extreme, I know. I'm not suggesting you all go out there and get inked, but, if you're still sitting on your sofa with that cuppa or glass of fizz (and I hope you are; you deserve it), then why not schedule in a moment to rest and explore some of the questions raised in this chapter in more detail? Ask yourself honestly whether you are getting enough time for prayer and Prosecco, selah and Sabbath, for time to energise yourself, and it will surely help you to thrive better.

Here are a few prompts to get you going.

- When do I get most rest? (Sleep doesn't count.)
- What drains me and how do I deal with that?

- What energises me? When do I actually do the things that energise me?
- Who can I talk to or go to for support – and do I?
- Who can I rest with/ have fun with/ be real with?

Helen's story

Revd Helen Wakefield-Carr is a URC minister and has been in ordained ministry for nine years. She is a single parent to two adopted boys, has been through adoption leave in the church and continues to manage the juggle of home, work and rest.

❝Being a single parent is hard work, but also so rewarding. Without a doubt, one of the hardest things to manage is the childcare juggle. Working out when to leave the children with friends or family is, I would say, *the* hardest part of my job as a parent and minister. It is difficult to find good childcare or babysitters and it is hard to decide when I should leave them – without feeling guilty. So you can imagine finding the time and headspace to rest is a nightmare!

Managing the balance between work and home can also be tricky, but the URC at synod and national levels have been amazing, giving me strong emotional support and some financial support too. I do have recommended working hours so, while I never say no to working extra when needed, I keep a track of the hours I work and then when it is school holidays I can take the time back; it's slightly OCD, I know, but ensures that I not only have time with the boys but also have time to rest alone.

Despite the difficult juggle, I know that motherhood is part of my ministry. I don't think God ever intended me to give birth, but God did intend me to be a mother! Sometimes when ministry feels a chore and hard work, the cosy feel of bedtime and having that quality time with my children reminds me that God has a plan for me, and my children are part of that plan. No one wanted to adopt them as they had a difficult background and social services were on the verge of separating them into different foster homes. Though life has been a challenge, it's when I see them peacefully asleep in bed that I wonder where they would be if we hadn't all found each other. They've brought something different to ministry life too. I had no idea how my relationships in the church and community would change; for example, people who would not work with me previously completely mellowed to my children. I have also made connections with people, due to having a child with additional needs, that I would not have met otherwise.

It's hard to find a way that works, balancing life as a ministry mum. I have never found a mother in the Church who I feel is the perfect model and maybe that's because we are trying to do an impossible job! However, I take comfort knowing that Jesus' ministry wasn't exactly easy or perfect either. Maybe those we deem to be "failures" (too busy, too disorganised, too tired) in ministry should be the ones we admire, as they are modelling real life!

So here are some suggestions that, for me, help and might also help you:

- planning and organisation
- listening to your children and giving them quality time, not snapshots of time
- not hesitating to cry, not hesitating to scream
- not thinking you're a bad mum if you need to sit in the garden on the swing and calm down before you carry on with cooking the tea
- never forgetting to keep on cuddling!

For me, the affection we have together is what grounds me in what is really important in life.**9**

Guilt management can be just as
important as time management
for mothers.

(SHERYL SANDBERG, 2015)

8

Distraction and defeat

WHEN IT ALL GETS TOO MUCH

Screeching up to school ten minutes late with a colleague on speaker phone plotting the week's events, I shoved my children into the car, waving furiously for them to be quiet so I sounded at least vaguely professional, and responded to the cries of 'we're hungry, did you bring a snack?' by frantically searching the glove box for a non-furry mint imperial or two.

This was not the first time that I recognised I was overly distracted – from work by the kids and from the kids by work.

One thing I've realised over the last few months is that trying to write a book while doing a six-days-a-week job and having a family is actually pretty foolish. I've sobbed at the keyboard, yelled at my husband, taken time off from work in order to write that I could have spent with the kids and suffered from anxiety for the first time in my life.

Don't get me wrong; I don't deserve any pity. It has been my choice, my husband has supported me writing and I felt God calling me to do it, but it has been tough and at times I have felt both defeated and distracted from the most important things in my life.

Perhaps the hardest thing I've had to deal with is guilt, hitting with a vengeance like never before, condemning every part of my life. I don't know about you, but, as a working mum, guilt is always there in the background, creeping into my thoughts and infesting my mind with negativity. Usually, I'm able to deal with it but recently it has begun to take hold. My mind races from guilt about not getting enough work done to guilt about not spending enough time with the kids; guilt about not fitting in a date night and not helping with the school PTA, to guilt that I haven't done the supermarket order. I feel guilty when I use Amazon Prime over going to the High Street; guilty when I have to take time off work because my child is ill *and* about taking time off when *I* am ill. Guilt takes over when I desperately want some time to myself (and about not wanting to spend *that* time with my husband/children), when I miss my son's hockey match or when I take five minutes for a cup of tea in a busy day. Basically I just feel guilty that I am not flippin' perfect. Guilt has at times brought me to my lowest point as a ministry mum, almost to defeat. Anyone else feel like this sometimes?

For you, it might not be guilt that brings you down; it might be that your mental health has suffered or you've been bullied at work; perhaps you have suffered grief and loss or disappointment. I wonder what challenges you have faced or are still facing. Whatever they are, probably most of us have faced, or will face, crises in our ministry mum lives that distract us from who we are and what we're called to, maybe even taking us to a point of defeat. In this chapter I want to take us through some of these difficult things and encourage us to think about how we can deal with the really tough stuff without getting defeated.

Mum guilt

I don't know if you've ever tried googling 'mum guilt'? I have; there are over 16 million results, filled with mums pouring out their guilt over everything from going back to work to giving their kids a bag of crisps! Every mum blog, book or Insta account I've seen talks about it. It's an epidemic, I tell you! I've not met one working mum who doesn't feel guilty about something.

When I was pregnant with my first child, a mere innocent in the ways of parenting, and simply enjoying my funky tie-dyed maternity dungarees (oh yes, I did, and I adored them, so shush yourself), a dear friend said to me that I would never have another worry-free day for the rest of my life. *Gee thanks,* I thought. *That's the way to make me feel good about being a parent.* But while she was right (there *is* always something with your kids to worry about) a more helpful comment might have been – and I feel this needs an echo and a loud booming voice – 'Youuuuu willllll alwayssss feeeeeel guiltyyyyyy.' It can be all-consuming.

Sheryl Sandberg, American technology executive, activist, author, mum and Chief Operating Officer of Facebook has a point when she says, 'Guilt management can be just as important as time management for mothers.'

Think about it – how much time do you spend worrying about your choices, your children, your work? Old decisions flare up; new decisions bring more opportunity for guilt to set in. I don't know about you, but guilt has been an unwelcome guest in my life for far too long, so if this sounds like you – join me – we really need to learn to manage our guilt.

I mean, listen, this is not the 1950s; it's OK that we, as women, go out to [*whispers*] work. As much as *some* of the older generation may at times question it, it really is not a big deal. We are not expected to swan around at home in a perfectly pressed and home-made day dress, while scrubbing the floor, darning socks and making jam that will keep us going all year (though I do confess to making some chutney just last week).

As a ministry mum, my actual daily life swings from an unclimbable washing mountain, where the summit is never reached; to the hand-holding of the dying, preparing for another's, perhaps unwanted, summit. Both are an absolute privilege (yeah OK – not really sure washing my kids underpants is a privilege) and yet I rarely feel that I am succeeding at either; it's more just about keeping the wheels on. I've missed so many things I think people have just stopped inviting me. Not only do I feel guilty I can't do these things, I *actually* can't do them, so I miss out doubly. Often the family can go to things I can't, so they get to have fun without me. Guilty, fear-filled thoughts entice me to wallow in them and condemn myself. As Vicki Psarias says in *Mumboss*, 2018:

> Guilt is a mother-f**ker. No one feels guilt like a mother. This is exacerbated by second-guessing yourself as a parent, when you endlessly question if your choices are the right ones. This, in turn, can lead to self-doubt in all areas of your life.

Oh my! Yes, guilt brings condemnation that infects my whole life. Plus, like many working mums, I also have to contend with the opinions of others adding to it. I really don't need someone else pointing out to me that I have missed an event at school that week or that they think 'I should spend more time with the children' or that their expectations of my life are not the same as my own. I have enough guilt of my own without you adding to it, thank you very much. If this sounds familiar, then let's remind ourselves that Paul writes in Romans 8.1, 'There is therefore now no condemnation for those who are in Christ Jesus.'

If God does not condemn us, why do we condemn ourselves? One thing we can do to manage the guilt and condemnation is to remind ourselves of our identity – you read chapter one, right? – first up, because for most of us we need to be reminded of this a lot! It's hard for condemnation to gain any kind of traction if we are solidly convinced of who we are and what we are called to do and be 'in Christ Jesus'.

Trauma, grief and burnout

It's not just guilt that can bring us to face defeat; perhaps one of the hardest things about any of this is having to deal with really difficult personal stuff, often in the public eye. Preaching forgiveness while you battle your own reluctance to forgive a deep-seated wound;

supporting those in grief while handling your own; facing the break-down of a relationship while attempting to manage the church; standing with those who are chronically ill while facing your own child's sickness; some of us will have faced these and more. Sometimes our church communities can be wonderfully supportive, giving us space, taking on things to relieve our load, providing practical help – meals, babysitting and more. I heard from one ministry mum who, after suffering a miscarriage, found her colleagues so supportive she was able to ease back in to work and to avoid difficult situations like toddler groups or baptism meetings until she felt ready. Sometimes, though, our colleagues and congregations are less understanding. Sometimes we find we need to hold in our pain in order to 'be professional', to protect others, and we put on a front and just keep going. Sadly, I've heard several stories of ministers being bullied by those in authority but unable to get help.

One ministry mum in the wider Anglican Communion, Anna (not her real name), shared with me some of her experience of what it's like to be gay, a single mum and a priest. She revealed she has had a difficult journey in the Church, one that even stopped her ministering for a while. There seemed to be a sense in the church around her that being a woman and gay made it almost impossible to minister. Thankfully, the joy of becoming a mum was a big part of bringing Anna back to ministry and she now ministers in her local parish whenever she can. However, the journey is immensely tough at times with, as she notes, many churches just not knowing how to acknowledge non-traditional families, and many families like hers facing a struggle just to be in church, let alone ministry. Anna sadly notes the choice she has felt necessary to make:

I have reluctantly come to accept that there is no foreseeable time when I will be able to be publicly in love. Normal things like sharing a home, being welcomed to a new ministry together or holding hands in a coffee shop are not going to happen.

Anna suggests that being a ministry mum brings tremendous joy and sadness at the same time, largely because at the heart of the struggle is that sense of two vocations in tension with each other – family and ministry.

Whatever the difficult situations we face, whether they come from our own guilt and condemnation, from others' criticism, from the trials we face, or simply from being in a constant state of tiredness and stress due to the nature of being a working parent, burnout is a real risk.

Working mum Michelle Obama, who knows all about the stress of public life as a parent, said in her 2018 autobiography:

Women, in particular, need to keep an eye on their physical and mental health, because if we're scurrying to and from appointments and errands, we don't have a lot of time to take care of ourselves. We need to do a better job of putting ourselves higher on our own 'to-do' list.

This is a particular concern for many working mums. One priest told me she feels that, in order to fulfil the expectations of her, she has to work harder than male colleagues to prove herself, while also being a perfect parent and doting wife.

St Luke's, an organisation that supports the physical and mental health of Anglican clergy, notes that:

Clergy are particularly vulnerable to accumulating excessive stress levels because of the nature of their job which includes multiple roles and responsibilities. The unrealistic expectations of others, the lack of boundaries associated with the role and often little collegial or line managerial support are also contributory factors.

As ministry mums, we face both of these demands – the expectations of being a minister and the pressures of being a mum – so might find ourselves at greater risk of burnout or defeat. Burnout can look like many different things, from physical exhaustion to mental health conditions, with *Psychology Today* noting in 2013 that it doesn't suddenly appear but gradually builds up with symptoms including insomnia, impaired concentration, increased anxiety and irritability, even anger, detachment, headaches and increased illness like colds and so on, as well as the obvious tiredness. What if the guilt, the condemnation and the anxiety take over? What if it all gets too much? What if we have to face burnout or defeat? What if our mental health is compromised? What if we just can't carry on?

First, it's OK.

You are not a failure.

You are not a bad minister.

You are not a bad mother.

You are loved.

Second, please don't just keep going on the basis that things might improve or that if you 'just get through this week' it will all be OK. That's exactly the time when you need to stop and rest (and not feel remotely guilty about it). A few years back, I suffered from chronic exhaustion and, although I'm largely well now, it means I have a heightened sense of when I am doing too much and I know that I can't ignore those warning signs. I recognise now that when I start to go down that path, I lose my perspective and get distracted. I start to doubt my calling, my effectiveness as a minister, my standard of motherhood. I question whether I can actually do it at all. When this happens, I know I need a few quieter days and not to even think about the long view until I've had some decent rest and can review things more calmly and rationally.

Learn to recognise when you are on a downward spiral – what are the triggers? Take a break when you need. Recognising your limitations is not a bad thing. In fact, being self-aware enough to know what you can sustain and what you can't, I think, says more about your integrity than it does about what you can't do. We've already looked at expectations and know that most ministry roles expect far more of the minister than is humanly possible and, even though we believe in a God of the impossible, we have to take some responsibility for ourselves too!

Keeping your mental health healthy

For some of us, mental health conditions will affect our lives, whether triggered by stress or burnout or by other means. As church leaders we are often assumed to be indestructible – after all we have a hotline to God, right? Isn't God going to keep us going, no matter what? The reality is that, according to the charity MIND, one in four people will suffer from a mental health condition of some sort during their life and as ministers we are not immune. Thankfully, as a society, we are much more open about mental health conditions now; it is easier to get help and support and you are much more likely to find people being compassionate and understanding than in the past.

However, in the church sphere, the spiritual question often raises its head. I know those who've been told they are possessed, don't have enough faith or are being deceived by the devil when they are diagnosed with a mental health condition. I was talking to a friend about this recently, who shared her own way of thinking about it: 'We live in a broken world and I have a broken brain. As a consequence of that, other parts of my life can be affected, such as my physical and spiritual health, and like any other illness, the devil uses it to pull me away from God.' I find her description helpful because she both recognises that there is something medically wrong, which she can seek help for, and acknowledges that her faith can be affected by the condition in a spiritual way.

Will van der Hart, of the Mind and Soul Foundation, takes a similar view, suggesting that everything in our lives has a spiritual element to it; that we are spiritual beings, created in God's image and living in a world in which the Spirit is at work. The result is that all situations in our lives are spiritual. For example, we could say that a common cold is spiritual – in other words it's not God's intention that there is illness of any kind and it won't be like that in heaven. But we wouldn't say, 'The devil has given me a cold.' That would be over-spiritualising the reality of our circumstance. We'd be better off taking some paracetamol and going to bed. We can look at mental illness in exactly the same way; that it is not what God had planned for us and in the same sense as anything else it *is* spiritual. But it is not 'more' spiritual than a physical illness and, just as we would take medication for a cold, we can treat the majority of mental health conditions through the use of medications and talking therapies.

Getting help

The long and the short of it is – get help if you need it! If you face any kind of distraction or defeat, don't let the overly spiritual crowd stop you getting the help you need in medication, therapy or support. Equally, though, keep praying. Every part of us is made, known and loved by God, so that includes our mind and our emotions. I find the Psalms can be really helpful here; the psalmist is often in despair or lament and the Psalter shows an absolute rollercoaster of emotion, so much so that some commentators have asked whether the psalmist may have suffered from bipolar disorder. We can't be sure, of course, but what we do see is the psalmist continually bringing his thoughts and feelings to the Lord in prayer. It can be hard for us not to turn away from God when we are struggling or suffering. All the good, positive spiritual habits we have built up can be torn down by the strength of the illness we face or the exhaustion of keeping it all going, or the burnout or the all-consuming guilt. But I want to encourage you to keep the lines of communication open between you and God, even if it is to share exactly what you think of the divine right now – I'm pretty sure God's heard worse!

I wish I could guarantee that when you seek help for whatever you are facing it will always be positive. Sadly, it isn't always, so if you are in a vulnerable place that is going to be difficult to handle, make sure you have key trusted people who you can share with, who know you and who can support you, no matter what. Often support is good and healthy and there to enable you to continue to do what you do without falling apart. There are some suggestions of places you can seek help in the further reading section at the back of this book.

The fear

Something I've realised over the last few years is that so many of us deal with fear. Guilt is largely the fear of the 'what if?' What might happen? What might people think? What might happen to my kids, my ministry and my life? It's all a hypothetical fear but can really drag us down. Carrying on regardless can come from a place of fearing what will happen if we say no, if we do less, or because we believe we are unable to stop, and so often leads to burn out. Mental health conditions can be exacerbated because we fear others' reactions if we are honest about our suffering or if we seek professional help.

Fear in this sense, the Bible tells us in 1 John 4, is about punishment, yet we believe in a God who took any punishment we might deserve on the cross. This passage also tells us in verse 18 that the God of unconditional love shows that 'perfect love casts out fear'. In this life, perhaps we receive just a glimpse of that, but one day that perfect love will drive all fear from us and we will live in absolute freedom. In the meantime, I question whether, when we are fearful and guilt-ridden, are we simply punishing ourselves? For me, I know this is so often the case; often it is not other people making me feel guilty or condemning me, but myself. How about you?

I wonder if Timothy had similar fears. In Paul's two letters to him there are pointers that all was not well with Timothy. It seemed people looked down on him because he was young, that he was surrounded by 'godless chatter' and was apparently in a rather challenging mission field. In Paul's second letter to him, he starts out by reiterating how much he loves him, how special his faith is and how he is part of a family legacy of those who know Jesus – Paul is building him up. Then he reminds him not to be afraid:

Therefore I remind you to stir up the gift of God which is in you through the laying on of my hands. For God has not given us a spirit of fear, but of power and of love and of a sound mind. (2 Timothy 1. 6–7 NKJV)

Not fear, but power, love and a sound mind.

Perhaps these might be useful tools for us too as we navigate our ways as ministry mums. When we fear the 'what ifs' or being sucked into a downward spiral, let's remember that, like Timothy, God has equipped us for the callings given to us. As Paul Coelho wrote in 1994, if we don't step into all we are, we might be asked, 'What have you done with the miracles that God planted in your days? What have you done with the talents God bestowed on you?'

I read this as a reminder to be the people God has made us to be, with all our gifts and talents. There is great power in knowing who we are and holding to it. That power can bring choice and guidance, reason and inspiration. I might ask myself, with one foot in the parenting camp and one firmly in the Church, am I challenging the ingrained attitudes that condemn and bring guilt or simply putting up with them? *I* have power to influence those around me, to gently bring to mind the unrecognised lenses through which people view the world; to point out the comments that wound 'unintentionally'; or the decisions which are formed with 'inadvertent' prejudice. God doesn't guilt-trip us into conforming; God gives us power to be who we are made to be!

Power and then: *love*. Love simply has to be the cornerstone of all we are and all we do. Paul says that without love he is just a clanging cymbal; he even says love is worth more than understanding all mysteries and knowledge, which sounds like a pretty big deal, really (1 Corinthians 13). If we can hold on to just how loved we are, whatever we face, whatever rubbish is thrown at us, we might find it easier to deal with fear, condemnation and difficult times. I know it's not easy – when we are in the middle of a crisis, when we are facing objection, when the proverbial is hitting the fan – that's why we need those around us to remind us, encourage and support us.

Love can also be our fuel when we face prejudice. Whenever I feel trampled underfoot, whenever another minister turns his back on me because of what's on my chest, whenever I am ignored, shouted down or belittled, whenever my own sisters in Christ accuse me of 'letting the side down', I can choose to respond in love. Love is the best bomb disposal unit ever invented. Have you seen how quickly a loving word can deflate a puffed-up angry chest?

Finally, *a sound mind.* A sound mind often seems far from me, when all around is blurring into one, when I start to preach the shopping list instead of my carefully crafted sermon – now in the clutches of my husband and his shopping trolley. For any of us, including those struggling with mental health conditions, that might sound like a kick in the teeth. God gave me a sound mind. Really? Yes, really. I think when Paul wrote this to Timothy he knew that Timothy was facing some tricky stuff. I think he was reminding him of his identity in Christ and not to be defined by what others were saying or the negativity he faced. We are all defined as children of God, no matter what. God gave each of us a mind to think, to process, to compute and, while we might recognise that the processes can be affected by anything we face, we also know that God doesn't waste anything. How many of us can cite examples of God being at work in the difficult things we've been through, giving us testimonies of God's love at work? For those of us with mental health conditions, we might know that our experiences have helped others, that in dark times God has brought out new gifts in us. In Ramona's story at the end of this chapter, you can read her account of God working in her through her bipolar diagnosis, for example.

Managing our well-being

Guilt management, mental health management, well-being management – whatever we call our own needs, keeping an eye on them is, without a shadow of a doubt, essential to our own health and welfare. I never imagined when my kids were a mere twinkle in my eye that one day I'd feel consumed with guilt about how I parent them. When I started out in ministry life, I never knew how much work could affect my own well-being. I never realised that I might get to the point of defeat. But I do now. I know when I start going down the condemnation route, that's when I need to reach out to someone who can ground me and remind me to shift my focus so I can once again stir up the gift of God which is within me. So, why not join me, the next time you question your ability as a mother or minister; the next time someone points a condemnatory finger at you; the next time the kids are clamouring for supper and there's just half a block of slightly old cheese and a squishy apple in the house; let's stir up in ourselves that 'God has given me a spirit of power, of love and a sound mind' and let's darn well use it.

Ramona's story
Revd Ramona Samuel has been a local Methodist preacher for many years, was ordained as a Methodist deacon three years ago and is now based in the Chelmsford Circuit. Ramona is married, has two children, aged 21 and 18, and was diagnosed with bipolar disorder two years ago.

❝I was 16 when I first felt a call to ministry but when I went to talk to my youth leader, the response was that I could either become a missionary or marry someone in ministry – leading over men was not an option for me as a woman.

I did go to Bible college years later and, after I got married, we moved to the UK from Antigua for my husband to study theology. We had children, he became a Methodist minister and through it all I still felt a strong pull towards ministry. I became a local preacher and it was at an "exploration day", years later, where I felt a connection with what deacons were doing. Part of my calling is about evangelism and working with people on the margins, and diaconal ministry felt closer to what I was feeling called to than presbyteral ministry.

My kids have grown up with their parents ministering in the Methodist Church and us sharing responsibility at home. When they were little, we always took them with us everywhere; they were easy children and would sit quietly and read books while we were ministering or at meetings. As they got older, it got tricky to navigate as we were often ministering in different places and we didn't want them to get turned off from church, so we decided to let them choose the church they would make their home. On the Sundays we didn't make it to church, they would often choose to hold services at home, dressing up and giving us Communion and my daughter would preach!

Things haven't always been easy, though. There has always been something different about my mental health. I was a "wild" child, totally extroverted and always doing weird and wonderful things; later in my teens I struggled but was very good at masking it. Then, about ten years ago, I reached defeat, having a big mental health crash, and was off work for five months. It felt like I had supressed it all for so long, but once it was out I couldn't control it any more and I had to explore what was going on. A few years ago I was finally diagnosed with bipolar disorder.

I have to manage the condition. I take medication and I draw, paint and do other creative stuff, as being creative helps me to cope. I also practice mindfulness. I'm very aware of my own self and take myself off to the doctors when I need to. They often ask: what keeps you from going under? I always answer: my faith.

In those really dark moments, I don't always think of praying – but I don't feel guilty about that because I look at prayer as being in God's presence and I think God is present with me all the time. Without faith my story would be very different. I think I've learnt to accept the condition and that it is part of who I am – a benefit of it is that it feeds my creativity.

The Methodist Church has been really supportive in it all; we have a well-being officer who I can tap into if I need and a counselling service too. In fact, I think the condition has strengthened my ministry. Before the diagnosis I questioned what was happening to me, wondering if I was a bad person, but in a way it's like the diagnosis has freed me to be who God has made me to be. I think I am more in touch with my creative side because of the condition, more in tune with my own frailty and therefore also probably more sensitive to other people as a result. I feel free to talk about it or mention it when I preach and I know being honest has helped other people too. '

My mission in life is not merely to survive, but to thrive; and to do so with some passion, some compassion, some humour and some style.

(MAYA ANGELOU)

Summary

Thronged by the thousands of tourists around us, I walked into Antoni Gaudí's world-famous basilica, with my kids and husband on either side. I'd visited it years ago as an arty teen, but stepping into the Sagrada Familia in Barcelona, I walked right into the presence of God. I wanted to fall to my knees in praise, abandoning myself in worship, but instead tried to find a quiet corner to get a grip! But Gaudí designed it as an open space – no hidden chapels, and even the labelled 'quiet zones' were filled with selfie-stick-toting gawpers. Finally, I found a few pews reserved only for prayer, in front of the altar. As I sat there, I found myself overwhelmed with a longing to preside at that altar, to stand there and share the truth of Jesus in word and in the bread and wine, in this glory-filled place. As God reminded me to be and do all I am called to, I felt a searing pain that as a woman and an Anglican I could not (likely never) stand behind that altar; it was as if someone were putting a knife into my destiny. That experience cemented in me my own path, but also reminded me of the pain which still exists in the Church, of the wounds that are still born both by those who minister and those as yet unable to. It is so important that, through the early years of ministry and motherhood to the Jesus Jenga Juggle, through the sacrifice, expectations and formation of new and unique ministry moulds, we never forget these moments, which remind us what we are called to and *who* is calling us to it. Don't be afraid to seek God afresh in that sense of calling or purpose. Often we hear people say things like, 'If God hasn't told you to do anything else, keep doing what was asked of you', but we might consider how often we actually ask the question of God or take time to listen to the answer.

As we hold tight to these moments of clarity, new and old, it is important that we move forwards with vision. We stand on the shoulders of those who have gone before: from Mary Magdalene sharing the news of the risen Christ, to Junia, Priscilla, Phoebe and other women who Paul highlighted in the early Church; from the monastery-founding St Hilda in the seventh century, to Jarena Lee in the nineteenth century, the first woman permitted to preach in the African Methodist Church; from Constance Coltman, the first female minister in the UK in the twentieth century, to Katharine Jefferts Schori, first female bishop in the Anglican Communion. These women and many others have tilled the ground for us. Not to do away with all that went before, but to make space for us to flourish alongside our male colleagues, to bring something 'other'. I love this quote from Maya Angelou: 'My mission in life is not merely to survive, but to thrive; and to do so with some passion, some compassion, some humour and some style.' I believe that, with Jesus' help, and the help of others around us, we can all *thrive* as ministry mums.

First, we can *thrive with passion*. Motivational speaker Simon Sinek once tweeted, 'Working hard for something we don't care about is called stress. Working hard for something we love is called passion.' We've probably all had mornings where the passion for the pillow might outweigh the excitement of the day ahead, but underneath the daily grind and the hard work, let's aim to be passionate about life and surround ourselves with those who fan this passion into flame. Two of my mates recently told me that they are going to be my cheerleaders, bringing pompoms everywhere I go. I really hope they are joking about the pompoms, but I love that they want to encourage me and cheer me on. Find those people who can pick you up when it's been a tough week; who you can text with a random prayer request; who you know will spur you on and energise you, not drain you. Michelle Obama recounts in her autobiography that her college advisor suggested dismissively that she was not 'Princeton material'. Instead of watering that seed of failure, she sought out someone who would support her and encourage her. Needless to say, a few months later she was offered a place – and she's not stopped thriving with passion since. And let's not assume passion needs to be BIG. Passion for you might be a *gentle* fire that burns beneath the surface, keeping you warm. John Wesley, founder of the Methodist Church, who travelled miles and miles on horseback and on foot, through every weather imaginable to preach the gospel, famously described his encounter with the Holy Spirit with the rather modest assertion that his heart felt 'strangely warmed'.

Second, we can *thrive with compassion*. As we've seen through the stories shared in this book, being a mum in ministry is entirely possible but can sometimes still be contested. We have to find our own way when confronted with negative opinions or condemnation – we each know what we find acceptable or not. In many ways I don't think we should have to 'put up with' any condemnation but I also know grace should be my springboard. Even Jesus got annoyed with those who didn't understand him, but he is known far more for his compassion. For me, if I hang on to the aim of thriving with compassion rather than anger, I know that I can fight gently where needed while pointing people to Jesus more than myself.

Third (and this one's vital!), we can *thrive with humour and style*. That uniqueness in our gifts and skills can be hard to hang on to sometimes, but there are countless examples of God using the things about us personally to reach others for the sake of the gospel. What's more, the humour I find littered throughout my life is one reason why I know God loves comedy; we all need those moments of farce to keep us topped up with joy. I will always remember sitting beside an older church member who had accidentally woken Siri on his device during a meeting that was dragging on, way past my kids' bedtime. I leant over to ask, 'Siri, when will this meeting end?' with Siri's tell-tale ping as she started to answer, sending us sniggering while he flustered to turn it off. Or the morning I had decided to have open house, finding myself in dog collar removing skid marks from the toilet two minutes before my guests were due to arrive, only to then notice the puddle of wee on the floor, which I was now kneeling in. *Boys.*

We can have all the passion, compassion, humour and style but if we aren't producing fruit, none of that matters. The Psalms remind me of this again and again, filled as they are with every possible emotion displayed in them. Psalm 92 highlights to me that need to be fruitful, with its focus on thanksgiving and pointing to the flourishing of those who love the Lord:

> The righteous flourish like the palm tree,
> and grow like a cedar in Lebanon.
> They are planted in the house of the LORD;
> they flourish in the courts of our God.
> In old age they still produce fruit;
> they are always green and full of sap,
> showing that the LORD is upright;
> he is my rock, and there is no
>   unrighteousness in him.
> (Psalm 92.12–15)

These few verses resound with a holy sales pitch: stick with God and you'll thrive; you'll be strong, you'll have longevity and energy and you'll be fruitful in what you do. In this we will reveal the Lord to those around us. These verses remind me to be ambitious for God's kingdom and that I am called to 'do' as well as 'be'. They ask questions like: do you see the fruit of God in your life? Where is God at work? In ministry, are we helping our congregations thrive? At home, are our families flourishing? Are you seeking God for the strength and energy you need to fulfil your God-given purpose?

We have work to do for God's kingdom. When we thrive, we can help others thrive; when we are fruitful, we help others to bear fruit also. The Church of England's 'Living Ministry' report published in 2018 is an ongoing research project looking into the well-being of clergy. While CofE-focused, it contains some interesting observations around ministry life in general. The report notes that

'Flourishing in [ordained] ministry incorporates two aspects: the flourishing of the person (well-being) and the flourishing of the ministry (ministerial outcomes). The two are inextricably intertwined.' Our flourishing depends on the flourishing of others. While looking for our own, it's important to keep thinking: how can we be a cheerleader or role model to others? I hope that this book can in many ways be a cheerleader to you, a reminder that *you can do it.*

This is not actually a book about feminism or one that suggests that 'the future is female'. This is a book about living out God's calling wholeheartedly. It's a book about women doing amazing things for the kingdom of God, ministering across the breadth and diversity of Christ's Church in so many different ways. It's a celebration of the women who have gone before us and a rally cry to those yet to come. It's a book for ministry mums who are battle-scarred and weary, and those who are just beginning to explore what a mutual calling might mean for them. It's a book which says we stand together and we will stand with those still fighting for their right to explore that calling. It's a book that wants to encourage and build up, which wants you to read it and say, 'We've got each other's backs'. It's a book that encourages you to throw yourself into this rising Holy Spirit-tide, washing through the bride of Christ and bringing a breath of fresh air in its wake. But, perhaps most importantly, it's a book powered by stories – mine, yours and the stories yet to be told. That's why this book ends with another story; but when you turn over the final page and step back into whatever you do next, I pray it will encourage you to write the next chapter of your own story with passion, compassion, humour and your own unique, irreplaceable, God-given style. After all, in the words of a Danish proverb, 'What you are is God's gift to you; what you do with yourself is your gift to God'.

Jo's story

Jo Read is an Assemblies of God Minister and Senior Pastor at Generations Church in Lincolnshire. She has been in ministry for

23 years, starting out as a youth pastor before going into senior church leadership. She is married and has two adopted children.

❝I've been in ministry with AoG for over 20 years and I've seen a lot of change in that time with many more women in leadership now than when I began. The national leadership has been instrumental in making a culture change in that respect but, as we have a lot of autonomy, many decisions are made at a local level. I'm really blessed to have been in a church that has been very releasing and I've been given a lot of scope to be the type of leader I was called to be. In fact, when our previous senior pastor left, it was the church elders who told me they wanted me to take over and that they weren't looking for anyone else.

One of the main cultural elements I've wanted to encourage at Generations Church is to be cross-generational (as the name suggests!) We encourage a culture of working together across the ages and forming partnerships between generations, which makes it much easier to be a leader with children. We've modelled this from the top down and as leaders we support each other and our families.

When we adopted our children, someone told me my kids would end up hating the Church and they'll blame you for it, but right then I made the choice to refute that. I love being in ministry and I want my kids to see that I view it as a privilege and an honour. We decided we were going to lead church as a family, so we've deliberately made our church a family focus. My husband works full-time as a teacher but serves at church at the weekends and we go along as a family to services and church events. We want our kids to grow up loving the house of God so we make it fun; they come to worship practice and sit in the PA cupboard (often with chocolate!) on occasion, or they help set out chairs and they do enjoy it. Of course they haven't hit teenage years yet, so I don't know what is to come!

One of the best bits of advice I was given about being a mum in ministry is to think about what the most important thing in your life is at any one time. God always comes first but then actually sometimes the rest can shift. If someone is seriously ill or dying, then they might be the most important thing in that moment and I'll go to them. At other times it's my family and they trump everything else and I say no to church. I find that this has been helpful to take the pressure off myself.

I've also found thinking about the rhythm of life helpful and that this can change in different seasons. Every family has a completely different rhythm; mine won't be the same as yours and what I can cope with or my kids can cope with will be different from others. There's no one-size-fits-all in ministry and sometimes finding what's right has been trial and error! I have found I have learned to listen to my children more closely about how they are feeling and cancel things if I need to – I want them to know how important they are.

We want our children's faith to grow too, so we let them know what we're praying for so they can also see the answers to prayer. A lot of the time they just want to watch *Alvin and the Chipmunks*, then all of sudden they ask something profound and for us the tea table has been the perfect place where we can talk about things with them.

You can do both: you can be a mum and a minister. Sometimes it's hard, of course, but I think if you can find what works for you, you can thrive in it all. 〞

Bibliography

Archbishop's Council (2018) 'Living Ministry: Negotiating well-being: Experiences of ordinands and clergy in the Church of England: Panel Study Wave 1', September (available online at: www.churchofengland.org/ministry-development).

Armstrong, Christine (2018) *The Mother of All Jobs: How to have children and a career and stay sane(ish)* (London: Bloomsbury Publishing).

Ash, Christopher (2016) *Zeal without Burnout: Seven keys to a lifelong ministry of sustainable sacrifice* (Surrey: The Good Book Company).

Baptists Together (2018) 'Becoming a Mother in Ministry' Baptist Guide (available online at: www.baptist.org.uk/mother).

Beard, Mary (2018) *Women & Power: A manifesto* (London: Profile Books).

Bessey, Sarah (2013) *Jesus Feminist: An invitation to revisit the Bible's view of women* (New York: Howard Books).

Bible Society (2018) 'Mums in ministry research' (available online at: www.christian-research.org/reports/recent-research/mums-in-ministry).

Bolz-Weber, Nadia (2015) *Accidental Saints* (Norwich: Canterbury Press).

Bourg Carter, Sherrie (2013) 'The tell tale signs of burnout . . . do you have them?', in *Psychology Today*, 26 November (available online at: www.psychologytoday.com/gb/blog/high-octane-women/201311/the-tell-tale-signs-burnout-do-you-have-them).

Brown, Brené (2018) *The Gifts of Imperfection: Let go of who you think you're supposed to be and embrace who you are* (Center City, MN: Hazelden).

Coelho, Paulo (1994) *By the River Piedra I Sat Down and Wept* (London: HarperCollins).

Coleman, Kate (2010) *7 Deadly Sins of Women in Leadership: Overcome self-defeating behaviour in work and ministry* (Birmingham: Next Leadership Publishing).

Coyne, Matt (2018) *Man vs Baby* (New York: Scribner).

Croft, Steven (2016) *The Gift of Leadership* (Norwich: Canterbury Press).

Devaney, Susan (2018) 'Why Bishop Sarah Mullally wants more women at the top in the Church', *Stylist* (available online at: https://stylist.co.uk/visible-women/bishop-sarah-mullally-first-female-change-women-church-london/214078).

Emma (2017) 'The gender wars of household chores: a feminist comic': *The Guardian*, 26 May (available online at: www.theguardian.com/world/2017/may/26/gender-wars-household-chores-comic).

Emma (2018) *The Mental Load: A feminist comic* (New York: Seven Stories Press).

Ephron, Nora (2008) *Heartburn* (London: Virago).

Equality and Human Rights Commission (2016) 'Pregnancy and maternity-related discrimination and disadvantage', Department for Business, Innovation and Skills, HM Government (available online at: https://assets.publishing.service.gov.uk/government/uploads/system/uploads/attachment_data/file/509500/BIS-16-145-pregnancy-and-maternity-related-discrimination-and-disadvantage-summary.pdf).

Ettus, Samantha (2016) *The Pie Life: A guilt-free recipe for success and satisfaction* (Los Angeles, CA: Ghost Mountain Books Inc.).

European Commission (2017) 'Working time directive', European Commission (available online at: http://ec.europa.eu/social/main.jsp?catId=706&langId=en&intPageId=205).

Evans, Rachel Held (2012) *A Year of Biblical Womanhood* (Nashville, TN: Nelson Books).

Hamilton, Bethany www.bethanyhamilton.com

Harrington, Kimberly (2018) *Amateur Hour: Motherhood in essays and swear words* (London: HarperCollins).

Kings Business School (2017) 'Effective ministerial presence and what it looks like in practice. Insights from the Experiences of Ministry Project 2011–17' (available online at: www.kcl.ac.uk/business/assets/PDF/Effective-Ministerial-Presence-Brochure-final.pdf).

Kirby, Katie (2016) *Hurrah for Gin: A book for perfectly imperfect parents* (London: Hodder & Stoughton).

Kivimäki, Professor Mika et al. (2015) 'Long working hours and risk of coronary heart disease and stroke', *The Lancet*, 31 October, 386(10005): 1739–46 (available online at: www.thelancet.com/journals/lancet/article/PIIS0140-6736(15)60295-1/fulltext).

Leach, Tara Beth (2017) *Emboldened: A vision for empowering women in ministry* (London: IVP).

Letts, Quentin (2015) 'I know just the vicar for my parish church. Pity he's fictional', *The Spectator,* 21 March (available online at: www.spectator.co.uk/2015/03/i-know-just-the-vicar-for-my-parish-church-pity-hes-fictional).

Macintyre, James (2017) 'Clergy burnout: Why stress affects church ministers, and what they can do about it', *Christian Today*, 20 July (available online at: www.christiantoday.com/article/clergy-burnout-why-stress-affects-church-ministers-and-what-they-can-do-about-it/110954.htm).

McKnight, Scot (2011) *Junia Is Not Alone* (Englewood, CO: Patheos Press).

Middleton, Jules (2015) 'A short guide to surviving "the discernment process" in the Church of England', *Apples of Gold* blog (available online at: www.pickingapplesofgold.com/discernment-guide).

Miller, Shelly (2016) *Rhythms of Rest* (Ada, MI: Bethany House Publishers).

Moore, Allison M. (2008) *Clergy Moms: A survival guide to balancing family and congregation* (New York: Church Publishing Inc.).

NCT (2019) 'Breast feeding and returning to work', NCT (available online at: www.nct.org.uk/life-parent/work-and-childcare/returning-work/breastfeeding-and-returning-work).

Obama, Michelle (2018) *Becoming* (New York: Viking).

Office for National Statistics (2018) 'Working and workless households in the UK: January to March 2018 research', ONS (available online at: www.ons.gov.uk/employmentandlabourmarket/peopleinwork/employmentandemployeetypes/bulletins/workingandworklesshouseholds/januarytomarch2018).

Page, Dr Sarah-Jane (2016) 'Altruism and sacrifice: Anglican priests managing "intensive" priesthood and motherhood', *Religion and Gender*, 19 February, 6(1): 47-63 (available online at: www.researchgate.net/publication/304366418_Altruism_and_Sacrifice_Anglican_Priests_Managing_'Intensive'_Priesthood_and_Motherhood).

Page, Dr Sarah-Jane (2017) 'Double scrutiny at the vicarage', in Reiemer, V. (ed.), *Angels on Earth: Mothering, religion and spirituality* (Bradford, Ontario: Demeter Press).

Parsons, Rob (2009) *Teenagers! What every parent has to know* (London: Hodder & Stoughton).

Percy, Emma (2014) *What Clergy Do: Especially when it looks like nothing* (London: SPCK).

Perez, Caroline Criado (2019) *Invisible Women: Exposing data bias in a world designed for men* (London: Chatto & Windus).

Psarias, Vicki (2018) *Mumboss: The honest mum's guide to surviving and thriving at work and at home* (London: Little, Brown Book Group).

Sandberg, Sheryl (2015) *Lean In: Women, work and the will to lead* (London: WH Allen; see also: www.leanin.org).

Sinek, Simon (2012) Tweet (available online at: twitter.com/simonsinek/status/174469085726375936?lang=en).

Threlfall-Holmes, Miranda (2015) *Teenage Prayer Experiment* (London: SPCK).

Turner, Sarah (2016) *The Unmumsy Mum* (London: Penguin Random House).

Williams, Hattie (2017) 'More women than men enter clergy training, latest figures show', *Church Times*, 27 September (available online at: www.churchtimes.co.uk/articles/2017/29-september/news/uk/more-women-than-men-enter-clergy-training).

Further reading and resources

In the research for this book, I read so many articles, books and papers that challenged me, encouraged me and made me belly laugh. If you want to go deeper, read a bit more, need some help or just find that you are not the only one living in a farce, here are some things from the Bibliography that I want to highlight, plus some other suggestions and sources of useful information.

On being a woman

Perez, Caroline Criado (2019) *Invisible Women: Exposing data bias in a world designed for men* (London: Chatto & Windus).

Beard, Mary (2018) *Women & Power: A manifesto* (London: Profile Books).

On being a mum

Emma (2018) *The Mental Load: A feminist comic* (New York: Seven Stories Press).

Harrington, Kimberly (2018) *Amateur Hour: Motherhood in essays and swear words* (London: HarperCollins).

Kirby, Katie (2016) *Hurrah for Gin: A book for perfectly imperfect parents* (London: Hodder & Stoughton).

On being a working woman in the Church

Bessey, Sarah (2013) *Jesus Feminist: An invitation to revisit the Bible's view of women* (New York: Howard Books).

Coleman, Kate (2010) *7 Deadly Sins of Women in Leadership: Overcome self-defeating behaviour in work and ministry* (Birmingham: Next Leadership Publishing).

Moore, Allison M. (2008) *Clergy Moms: A survival guide to balancing family and congregation* (New York: Church Publishing Inc.).

Page, Dr Sarah-Jane (2016) 'Altruism and sacrifice: Anglican priests managing "intensive" priesthood and motherhood', *Religion and Gender*, 19 February, 6(1):47–63 (available online at: www.researchgate.net/publication/304366418_Altruism_and_Sacrifice_Anglican_Priests_Managing_'Intensive'_Priesthood_and_Motherhood).

Project 3:28 Database: www.project328.info (database of Christian female speakers).

W.A.T.C.H.: https://womenandthechurch.org (national organisation working actively for gender justice, equality and inclusion in the Church of England).

Women in Theology blog: https://womenintheology.org

Young Clergy Women: https://youngclergywomen.org (international network of young ordained women).

On being a working mum

Armstrong, Christine (2018) *The Mother of All Jobs: How to have children and a career and stay sane(ish)* (London: Bloomsbury Publishing).

Ettus, Samantha (2016) *The Pie Life: A guilt-free recipe for success and satisfaction* (Los Angeles, CA: Ghost Mountain Books Inc.).

Lean In: www.leanin.org (helping women support each other and achieve their goals).

Maternity leave and pay advice from the UK Government: www.gov.uk/maternity-pay-leave

Psarias, Vicki (2018) *Mumboss: The honest mum's guide to surviving and thriving at work and at home* (London: Little, Brown Book Group).

Working Families Organisation: www.workingfamilies.org.uk

Vocation

Middleton, Jules (2015) 'A short guide to surviving "the discernment process" in the Church of England', *Apples of Gold* blog (available online at: www.pickingapplesofgold.com/discernment-guide).

When you need support

Churches' Ministerial Counselling Service: www.cmincs.net (counselling for church ministers across a range of denominations)

Clergy Support Trust: www.clergysupport.org.uk (supporting Anglican clergy and their families).

MIND: www.mind.org.uk (the mental health charity).

Mind and Soul Foundation: www.mindandsoulfoundation.org (articles, support and guidance on mental health from a Christian perspective.)

Sheldon Hub: www.sheldonhub.org (a safe online place for people in ministry to share together).

St Luke's Healthcare: www.stlukeshealthcare.org.uk (a charity that aims to improve clergy health and well-being).